the *flexible* family cookbook

JO PRATT

PHOTOGRAPHY BY MALOU BURGER

F
FRANCES
LINCOLN

Contents

Introduction

It's a fact that most parents these days cook multiple meals at meal times, due to a rise in dietary requirements. It might be down to gluten and dairy intolerances; it could be for moral or environmental reasons; not to mention people just wanting to be more healthy and reduce the amount of meat, sugar or saturated fat they eat.

It's exhausting just thinking about it, and all of this has made eating together a little anti-social, as cooking to cover lots of requirements has become hard work. We all need easier ways to put food on the table and sadly many people will turn to ready-meals or takeaways as a solution.

Eating together as a family is such an important occasion. When you eat together, it's the perfect opportunity to catch up, relax, get things off your chest and generally have a good time. It is crucial, especially with all the pressures that our children are put under these days that there's a window to chat together and put things into perspective. I'm not saying we should be eating together for every meal of the day of course – one would be ideal, or even a just a few times during a week, be that a Sunday lunch, Friday night or even a Saturday brunch.

So, what I want to bring to you through this book is a variety of family friendly recipes that can be used for cooking balanced, nutritious meals to suit a variety of requirements. Recipes that include a number of flexible options so they're suitable for everyone to eat together. Think of it as the Swiss army knife of cookbooks. A multi-tool to provide practical recipe solutions for the demands and challenges of modern family life. You'll see that I've given a fairly healthy approach to many of the recipes, maximising the use of fresh and beneficial ingredients. I've also cut down on sugars where possible and used good fats and oils. But, I hasten to add, this is not a typical 'healthy eating' book. There are many 'naughty but nice' recipes in here. I am a believer in eating everything in moderation!

It's split into seven chapters: Breakfasts and brunch, Soups and broths, Small plates and snacks, Main meals, Sides, Baking and desserts, and finishing with a Dietary index.

Breakfast and brunch

This chapter includes a welcome range of recipes for the fast and furious mornings such as Breakfast Power Smoothie and super healthy Cocoa Granola; and the chilled out mornings, like Loaded Burritos, and Crispy Bacon and Halloumi on Avocado Toast – I couldn't possibly have a breakfast chapter without the obligatory avocado on toast recipe could I?

Soups and broths

The amazing thing about soup and broth is that they have the ability to serve so many purposes – comforting and hearty (Roast Tomato and Lentil with Halloumi Croutons), convenient (Simple Pho), clever and nutritious (Creamy Pea, Spinach and Cashew) and fun and quirky (Mexican Street Corn and Prawn Chowder). Here you'll find soups and broths are a great way of packing veg into your diet and one of the most flexible meal types around. Does anyone know the difference between a soup and a broth?

Small plates and snacks

The collection of recipes in this chapter are not only designed to be flexible with the ingredients you use, but also how or when you serve them. Whether it's a savoury snack post-school you need (Cheesy Cornbread Muffins are ideal), a light lunchtime platter (Danish Crackers with Tuna Spread and Pickled Cucumber), a stress-free starter (Spiced Chickpea Fritters), weekend sharing food for the family (Souvlaki Pitta Pockets), simple yet impressive party food (Popcorn Cauliflower Bites) or a cooking activity for the kids to get involved in (Chicken Noodle Spring Rolls).

Main meals

This chapter is packed with many low-maintenance one-pot meals and traybakes, making preparation and clearing up easy. Chicken Tinga with Watermelon Salsa is a brilliant sharing food for afterschool hangouts, or the Tikka Traybake is delicious for Friday night curry night and, my Tuscan Bean and Sausage Stew is just what you need for a hearty comforting supper at the end of a crazy week. You'll also find handy meals that can be prepared up to a certain stage and finished off for individual eating (such as Moroccan Baked Fish in a Bag or Prawn Laksa Parcels).

Sides

Forget chunks of cucumber or a bowl of peas to offer as a token veg, this chapter has plenty of creative and seasonal side dishes to serve with your main course. You'll also see many can be tweaked to become main meals.

Baking and desserts

Baking in particular can really start to bring on the challenges. Gluten, eggs and dairy are the backbone to many recipes. Luckily there are some fantastic alternatives available such as flours, plant-based milks and butters and even egg substitutes. I have included many recipes that would be suitable for most dietary restrictions, such as the Chocolate Celebration Cake or Lemon and Raspberry Loaf, but as and when required, there are numerous flexible options for you to choose that don't compromise taste in the slightest, such as swapping the eggs for chia seeds in the Sticky Lemon and Orange Cake – I challenge anyone to spot the difference.

Dietary index

This is a valuable time-saving section to refer to if you want to locate recipes that are suitable for specific requirements, whether it's vegan, vegetarian, pescatarian, dairy-free, gluten-free, nut-free or sesame-free.

So, in a (non-allergenic) nutshell – you'll find the recipes are simple, easy and convenient. Speed is key, straightforward methods are vital, so that anyone can follow them, and all dishes use ingredients that can be bought easily. The book is full of tips to make your life easier and I hope you find that it lives up to its title of being flexible and that your family and friends enjoy the ideas as much as my family and friends do. Whether it's your teenage daughter who has chosen to go vegan, a friend of your son who's coming for a sleepover with a sesame allergy, or your best friend who has a dairy intolerance, reach for this book and enjoy the results.

Be flexible! Jo x

breakfast and brunch

Flexible porridge toppers

Time taken 15 minutes / **Makes** 2 portions

Porridge or oatmeal as it's often called, is one of the most nutritious breakfasts we could start the day with and it's so simple to make. Generally speaking it's 1 part oats cooked with 3 parts liquid, whether using water or milk (dairy or alternative) or a combination of the two. Bring to a fast simmer and cook for a few minutes until thick and creamy. Serving it sprinkled with sugar, honey or syrup is a popular choice, but why not be a bit more creative and try some of these toppings.

Sticky pear and ginger

Peel, core and chop 2 ripe pears. Finely slice or chop 1 ball of stem ginger (from a jar). Heat a small saucepan and add the pears with 2 tablespoons ginger syrup from the jar, a pinch of ground cinnamon and 2 tablespoons orange juice or water. Cook over a medium-high heat for a minute or two until the pears are starting to soften and become sticky. Spoon on top of 2 bowls of hot porridge.

Flexible: switch the pear for apple or fresh figs.

Coconut, lime and mango

Sprinkle some coconut sugar over the top of 2 bowls of hot porridge. Top with diced mango, grate over the zest of ½ lime and scatter over some toasted coconut flakes. This is really nice if the porridge is made with ½ coconut milk and ½ water.

Flexible: go totally tropical and use pineapple, kiwi, papaya and passion fruit with the mango.

Chocolate syrup, banana and pecan

Put 3 tablespoons agave syrup in a small saucepan and stir in 2 teaspoons cocoa powder. Gently heat together until the cocoa is completely dissolved into the syrup. Top 2 bowls of hot porridge with sliced banana, drizzle over the chocolate syrup and scatter over some pecan nuts. This chocolate syrup can easily be made in larger quantities, left to cool and kept covered, at room temperature, for weeks.

Flexible: the syrup can also be added to milkshakes, ice cream or used as a dip for fruit kebabs. Warming some bought caramel sauce with a pinch of salt is a delicious alternative to making the chocolate syrup.

Honey and rose water apricots with pistachios

Put 8–10 dried apricots, cut in half, in a saucepan with 2 tablespoons honey and 4 tablespoons water. Bring to a simmer and cook for 5 minutes to soften the apricots and reduce the liquid to about 3 tablespoons. Remove from the heat. Cool to room temperature and add a few drops of rose water to the honey syrup to taste. Spoon the apricots and syrup on top of 2 bowls of hot porridge and scatter with chopped pistachio nuts.

Flexible: figs or dates can be used instead of apricots. You can also swap the rose water for orange blossom water.

Tahini, honey and fig

Mix together 2 tablespoons tahini, 2 tablespoons honey and 1–2 tablespoons hot water until you have a loose sauce. Cut 2–4 fresh figs into quarters and use raw or briefly fry them in a little butter until golden. Sit on top of 2 bowls of hot porridge and spoon over the tahini and honey sauce.

Flexible: sliced banana, ripe pear, blueberries or blackberries are great alternatives to the figs.

Nut butter, jam and apple

Use any nut butter you wish, such as peanut, almond or cashew. Try and match or complement it by using ½ quantity of nut milk to make the porridge. Top 2 bowls of hot porridge with a swirl of nut butter, a spoon of jam and finish by grating over ½–1 red-skinned apple.

Flexible: grated pear or sliced banana can be used instead of the grated apple. Finish with some toasted flaked almonds or coconut for added crunch.

13 / breakfast and brunch

Breakfast power smoothie

As much as I've tried, I just can't get my kids to enjoy porridge. It's such a shame since oats are a fantastic form of slow-release energy and a far better way to start the day than a bowl of sugary cereals. So, I tend to hide the oats in something I know they'd enjoy. This isn't for every day, but for when we're in a hurry. This is super-quick to prepare and will always get a thumbs-up from the kids.

20g/¾ oz porridge oats (gluten-free)

25g/1 oz cashew nuts

50ml/1¾ fl oz natural yoghurt

1 ripe banana, peeled and broken into pieces

125ml/4 fl oz/½ cup cold milk

1 tbsp maple syrup

½ tsp vanilla extract or vanilla bean paste

Time taken 5 minutes / **Makes** 1

Place all the ingredients in a blender and blitz for about 30–60 seconds (depending on the power of your blender) until completely smooth.

Enjoy straightaway or keep chilled until needed.

Flexible

Dairy-free/vegan: *use a dairy-free yoghurt and milk of your choice.*

Nut-free: *switch the cashew nuts for a raw egg. Not only will this provide the protein boost but it will make the smoothie super creamy.*

Get ahead: *this will sit in the fridge quite nicely if you prefer to make this overnight. You may just want to stir in a little extra milk if it thickens when sitting.*

Raspberry and mango smoothie

*This is my sneaky way of giving everyone a
good dose of fruit in a glass, but for an added
bonus, I've included some chia seeds. They
don't make any difference to the flavour and
give a great boost of calcium, protein, fibre
and omega-3 fatty acids, which is ideal for
those family members who don't, or should
I say 'won't', eat much fish in their diet.*

150g/5½ oz fresh or frozen raspberries
1 large ripe mango, peeled and roughly chopped
1 ripe banana, peeled and roughly chopped
juice from 2 oranges
2 tsp chia seeds

Time taken 10 minutes / **Makes** 2

Place all the ingredients in a blender and blitz for about
30–60 seconds (depending on the power of your blender)
until completely smooth. The smoothie is naturally quite
thick, so add some ice or cold water to loosen if you prefer.

Pour into a couple of glasses and serve straightaway.

Flexible

*Upgrade: add 100ml / 3½ fl oz natural yoghurt
(dairy or dairy-free).*

Iced banana and peanut butter smoothie

*This takes minutes to throw together, is
wonderfully healthy – and tastes like ice
cream… that's a treble win in my book!
You do need to think ahead with this though
and pre-freeze your bananas. My best bit of
advice here is to buy some over-ripe bananas
next time you see some, and freeze them
straightaway. Simply peel and roughly chop
first and store in a container.*

1 frozen banana, roughly chopped
175ml/6 fl oz/²/₃ cup cold milk
1 heaped tbsp peanut butter
1 Medjool date, stoned
½ tsp ground cinnamon

Time taken 5 minutes / **Makes** 1

Place all the ingredients in a blender and blitz for about
30–60 seconds (depending on the power of your blender)
until completely smooth.

Pour into a glass and serve straightaway.

Flexible

*Dairy-free: use a dairy-free milk of your choice such
as soya, almond or coconut milk.*

*Upgrade: add 1 teaspoon cocoa powder to the blender
for a chocolate twist.*

Cocoa granola

You can buy an amazing variety of granolas but they tend to be pretty pricey and loaded with sugar. Homemade granola may sound like it's going to be hard work but, believe me, this really isn't. You just need to stock up on a few basics next time you shop, and you'll end up with a nice big jar full of healthy goodness that you can dig straight into when you all get up.

————————————————

4 tbsp coconut oil, melted

4 tbsp maple syrup

2 ripe bananas, peeled

50g/1¾ oz Medjool dates, stoned

4 tbsp cocoa powder, sieved

2 tsp ground cinnamon

pinch of flaked sea salt

250g/9 oz porridge oats (gluten-free)

100g/3½ oz pecan nuts, roughly chopped

75g/2¾ oz dried cherries, raisins, sultanas or cranberries

50g/1¾ oz coconut flakes

50g/1¾ oz sunflower seeds

2 tbsp flaxseed

Time taken 1¼ hours / **Makes** 8–10 portions

Preheat the oven to 140°C/120°C fan/275°F/gas 1. Line a large baking tray with baking parchment.

Put the coconut oil, maple syrup, bananas and dates in a food processor or blender and blend to a smooth purée, then transfer to a large bowl.

Add the remaining ingredients and mix well, making sure everything is coated in the puréed mixture.

Tip onto the baking tray and loosely spread into a single layer. Bake for 1 hour, mixing the granola around every 15 minutes, breaking up any particularly large chunks.

After 1 hour the granola will still remain soft but will have a delicious toasted aroma and appear more golden brown. Remove from the oven and leave to cool. As it cools, it will become crisp and crunchy.

Once cool, store in an airtight container for up to 4 weeks – though it's highly unlikely it will last that long!

Flexible

Nut-free: omit the pecan nuts and replace with some additional dried fruit, such as banana chips, chopped figs, apricots or mango.

Upgrade: once out of the oven, let the granola cool for 10 minutes before stirring in 100g / 3½ oz dark chocolate chips or chunks, so they start to melt into the granola.

Sweet pastry twirls

Ready-rolled puff pastry is so handy when in need of a quick fix. Here I'm using it to make freshly baked breakfast treats for all the family to enjoy. These are my favourite three fillings but have a play around with your own flavours. For anyone with a late riser in the house (yes teenagers, you know who you are!), once prepared they can be kept in the fridge and cooked when needed so they are eaten warm.

375g/13 oz sheet of ready-rolled
   puff pastry
1 egg, beaten
2 tbsp caster (superfine) sugar

Cinnamon, pear, pecan and maple
For each twirl:
¼ ripe pear, peeled, cored and
   thinly sliced
1 tsp maple syrup
large pinch of cinnamon
2–3 pecan nuts, chopped

Raspberry, apple and almond
For each twirl:
1 tsp raspberry jam
¼ small eating apple, peeled, cored
   and thinly sliced
few toasted flaked almonds

Nutty chocolate banana
For each twirl:
1 heaped tsp chocolate and
   hazelnut spread
¼ banana, thinly sliced

Time taken 45 minutes / **Makes** 8 individual twirls

Preheat the oven to 200°C/180°C fan/400°F/gas 6. Line 8 holes of a muffin tin with non-stick muffin cases or strips of baking parchment (about 10–12cm/4–4½ inches). Alternatively, and even better, if you are using a silicone muffin tray you won't need to use anything to line the holes.

Remove the pastry from the fridge for 5 minutes before un-rolling and cutting widthways into 8 strips.

Spread, scatter, sprinkle or arrange your chosen fillings on top of each pastry strip. Roll each one up loosely to form a coil, and sit in the muffin tin holes. Brush the top of the pastry and any edges you can see with the beaten egg and scatter a little sugar over the top of each one for a golden top.

Bake for 20–25 minutes until the tops are wonderfully golden brown. Cool slightly before removing and serving warm or at room temperature.

Flexible

Vegan: unless you are using 'all-butter' puff pastry, most bought, ready-rolled puff pastries are vegan. To replace the egg glaze, you can use some sunflower oil to brush over the pastry twirls before baking.

Gluten-free: simply opt for buying a gluten-free puff pastry.

Flavour swap: spread a little tomato purée onto a pastry strip. Scatter with some grated cheese such as Gruyère or Cheddar and top with chopped ham. Roll up and cook as above.

Crispy halloumi and bacon

on avocado toast

No breakfast chapter in a cookbook would be complete without an avocado toast recipe! And all for good reason; avocado is super healthy and a versatile ingredient that holds itself well when chopped, mashed, sliced, raw, cooked, left plain or spiced up.

I've decided to keep things simple here by mashing the avocado and using it as a base to an open toasted sandwich topped with moorish crispy bacon and halloumi. If you're feeling extra hungry then sit an extra piece of toast on top.

---

2 large ripe avocado

2 tbsp pumpkin seeds

extra virgin olive oil

8 rashers streaky bacon, cut into
   thin pieces

250g/9 oz halloumi, diced into
   small cubes

4 slices sourdough, or alternative bread

flaked sea salt and freshly ground
   black pepper

Time taken 20 minutes / **Serves** 4

Scoop the avocado flesh into a bowl and roughly mash. Season with salt and pepper. Set aside.

Heat a frying pan over a medium-high heat. Add the pumpkin seeds and toss them around in the pan until they are lightly toasted and crunchy. Remove from the pan and return the pan to the heat.

Add a trickle of olive oil and the bacon. Fry for a few minutes until the bacon is golden and crisp. Remove with a slotted spoon and set aside.

Add the halloumi to the pan and fry for just a few minutes until it's golden. Meanwhile, toast the bread.

Drizzle olive oil over the toast and top with the avocado. Divide the halloumi, bacon and pumpkin seeds between the avocado toasts. Drizzle over some olive oil, add a twist of pepper and serve.

Flexible

Vegetarian: *instead of bacon, fry a handful of sliced chestnut mushrooms in olive oil, until golden and tender.*

Vegan: *cook mushrooms as above and for an alternative to the halloumi, use 150g/5½ oz tinned chickpeas, pat dry with kitchen paper and fry over a high heat in 1 tablespoon olive oil until lightly golden. Toss in ½ teaspoon sweet smoked paprika. Remove from the pan, then serve on the avocado toast with the mushrooms.*

Loaded breakfast burritos

These Mexican-inspired tortilla wraps will please anyone who is handed one. Often on a weekend I'll make these when we're all heading to various sporting or social activities, though each will vary slightly – one without cheese, one extra spicy, one with beans rather than chorizo (see 'flexible' tip below) and one loaded with everything. The preparation workload is the same, everyone is happy, feeling full and ready to tackle the day ahead.

---

1 tbsp olive oil

200g/7 oz cooking chorizo, thickly sliced

4 corn or wheat tortillas

knob of butter

6–8 spring onions (scallions), chopped

6–8 eggs, lightly beaten

1 tbsp chopped coriander (cilantro)

pinch of flaked sea salt

100g/3½ oz grated Cheddar cheese

75g/2¾ oz sweetcorn

1 large ripe avocado, diced

hot chipotle sauce or chilli flakes
  (optional)

Time taken 25 minutes / **Serves** 4

Heat the olive oil in a frying pan. Add the chorizo and cook for about 3–4 minutes until the slices are cooked through and are becoming golden.

Heat the tortillas over a gas flame, in a hot dry frying pan or hot griddle until they are lightly charred, and keep warm.

In a separate non-stick pan, melt the butter over a medium heat and add the spring onion. Cook for 2 minutes until softened. Add the beaten eggs, coriander and season with salt. Stir around in the pan until the egg is softly scrambled. Stir through the Cheddar until it's starting to melt then add the sweetcorn.

Divide the chorizo and cheesy scrambled eggs between the centre of each tortilla. Top with some avocado and add some chipotle or chilli flakes if using. Fold the top and bottom sides of the tortilla over the filling, then roll up to seal and hold in the filling. If you are planning on eating these on the go, wrap in foil or paper and twist the ends to secure. Cut in half and eat whilst hot.

Flexible

Vegetarian: *for every portion of a chorizo-free burrito, melt a knob of butter in a frying pan. Add a big pinch of hot or sweet smoked paprika and ¼ teaspoon ground cumin. Sizzle for a few seconds before adding around 75g/2¾ oz canned black beans or kidney beans. Toss to coat in the butter, heat through and season.*

Alternatively, you can heat up some canned baked beans with a pinch of smoked paprika stirred through.

Gluten-free: *opt for gluten-free tortilla bread. Make sure you check the chorizo is gluten-free too.*

Fruity oat pancakes

Weekends aren't complete in our house without pancakes. As much as the kids love the big crêpe-style pancakes, they'll always top them with the same thing (golden syrup for Rosa, and chocolate and hazelnut spread for Olly). To vary things and bring in some more nutritional goodness I like to make smaller, thicker American-style pancakes, flavouring them with fruits and using different flours and toppings. Serve them hot drizzled with syrup or honey and extra blueberries and slices of banana.

—————————————

100g/3½ oz porridge oats (gluten-free)
2 tsp baking powder (gluten-free)
125ml/4 fl oz/½ cup oat milk
2 eggs
1 ripe banana, peeled and roughly
    chopped
1 tsp vanilla bean paste
150g/5½ oz blueberries
2–3 tbsp sunflower oil

To serve
maple syrup, honey, agave or
    golden syrup
blueberries
sliced banana

Time taken 30 minutes / **Makes** 4–6 large or 10–12 small pancakes

Put the oats and baking powder into a blender or food processor and blitz until powdery like flour.

Add 100ml/3½ fl oz of the oat milk and the eggs, banana and vanilla, and blend until you have a smooth thick batter. The consistency needs to be able to drop off a spoon and not spread too far in the pan. Add the additional 25ml/1 fl oz oat milk if needed. Stir in the blueberries.

Heat a large pancake or frying pan over a high heat. Once the pan is hot, reduce the heat to medium and add a good drizzle of the oil. Swirl to cover the base of the pan and then dollop spoonfuls of the batter into the pan.

Cook for a couple of minutes or so until small bubbles appear on the surface around the blueberries. Carefully flip each pancake over and cook for a further minute. Keep the pancakes warm while you cook the remaining pancakes in the hot oiled pan until all the mixture has been used.

Serve hot drizzled with your choice of syrup, honey or agave and sprinkle with extra blueberries and slices of banana.

Flexible

Vegan/egg-free: the eggs can be replaced with ground flaxseed. Simply mix 2 tablespoons ground flaxseed with 6 tablespoons water. Leave to sit for 15 minutes to thicken and become gel-like. Add to the pancake mixture as you would the eggs.

Other fruits: blueberries can be replaced by all sort of soft fruits, fresh or frozen, such as raspberries, blackberries, chopped strawberries, halved and pitted cherries or sliced banana.

Chocolatey: for chocolate fans, you can add 2 tablespoons cocoa powder when making the batter. You may need to add a splash more oat milk if it seems a little too thick. Banana works well with the chocolate pancakes.

Power pancakes

with popped tomatoes

Pancakes don't always have to be the sweet version at breakfast time – savoury ones can be just as satisfying and I urge you to give these a go just to appreciate how fantastic they are. They are fuelled with chickpea flour and silken tofu, making them high in protein, low in carbohydrate and brilliant for anyone who's vegan, where pancakes are often off limits. Enjoy plant power at its best!

For the pancakes

200g/7 oz silken tofu

250g/9 oz gram (chickpea) flour

2 tsp baking powder

1 tsp flaked sea salt

250ml/9 fl oz/1 cup milk of your choice

2 tbsp olive oil

For the tomatoes

2 tbsp olive oil

400g/14 oz cherry tomatoes

2 tsp caster (superfine) sugar

2 tsp balsamic vinegar

pinch of dried chilli flakes (optional),
   plus extra, to serve

To serve

150g/5½ oz crumbled feta or vegan
   alternative (optional)

Time taken 20 minutes / **Serves** 4

To make the pancakes, simply blend all the ingredients, apart from the oil, until you have a thick smooth batter.

Heat a large pancake or frying pan over a high heat. Once the pan is hot, reduce the heat to medium and add a good drizzle of the oil. Swirl to cover the base of the pan and then spoon or ladle the batter to create pancakes of about 8cm/3¼ inch in diameter.

Cook for a couple of minutes or so until small bubbles appear on the surface. Carefully flip each pancake over and cook for a further minute. Keep the pancakes warm while you cook the remaining pancakes in the hot oiled pan until all the mixture has been used.

Meanwhile, to cook the tomatoes, heat another frying pan over a high heat and add the olive oil. Add the tomatoes and toss around for a few minutes until the skins burst and the tomatoes start to 'pop' open, releasing tomatoey juices. Sprinkle over the sugar, balsamic vinegar and chilli flakes, if using. Move around in the pan for a couple of minutes to continue softening the tomatoes but remove from the heat before they totally break down and they still retain some shape.

Serve the pancakes on plates, spoon over the tomatoes and finish with a scattering of chilli flakes and feta cheese, if using.

Flexible

Upgrade: once the tomatoes are cooked, remove from the pan. Return the pan to a high heat, add a good handful of baby spinach leaves and splash of water per person. Stir around until the spinach has wilted. Season and serve on the plate with the pancakes and tomatoes, drizzled with some tahini.

Keep it simple: the pancakes are delicious served as a snack with some hummus, cucumber and cherry tomatoes. Great for using up any uneaten pancakes later in the day.

Spice it up: the pancakes are delicious made with the addition of 2 teaspoons mild curry powder added to them and served as an accompaniment to all types of curries or dahls.

Chia-berry jam

Most households have a pot of fruity jam on the go for breakfast. As tasty as jam is, it's more often than not packed full of refined sugar which helps set the jam but doesn't provide nutritional goodness. This homemade jam recipe is the total opposite. I'm using chia seeds as an alternative to sugar. They absorb several times their size in liquid, creating a jelly-like texture that will set like jam.

500g/1 lb 2 oz fresh or frozen raspberries
1 tbsp lemon juice
1 tsp vanilla bean paste
4 tbsp agave, honey or maple syrup,
  or more to taste
3 tbsp chia seeds

Time taken 20 minutes / **Makes** about 600ml/1 pint/2½ cups

Put the raspberries, lemon, vanilla and 4 tablespoons of your chosen sweetener into a saucepan. Cook on a low-medium heat until the fruits have broken down to a pulp and released their juices.

Stir in the chia seeds and cook over a low heat for 10 minutes, stirring a couple of times throughout.

Have a taste and add more of your chosen sweetener if you feel it needs it. Some raspberries will be naturally sweeter than others, depending on the time of year. Leave to cool in the pan and then spoon into a sterilised jar.

Once cold, store in the fridge and use within 1 week, or alternatively freeze for up to 3 months and defrost before using.

Flexible

Other fruits: *you can swap the raspberries for all sorts of fruits such as strawberries, blackberries, blueberries, cherries, or even do a combination of fruits. I'll grab a bag of mixed fruit from the freezer and use that when fresh fruits are out of season.*

Seedless: *for those who are fussy about seeds in their jam, you can blend the cooked jam, breaking down any raspberry and chia seeds before transferring into jars.*

soups and broths

Tortellini minestrone

Making a pot of minestrone is the perfect time to use up the veggies that you intended on using for something else, and didn't quite get round to. Don't let them turn to mush at the bottom of your fridge drawer.

Small pieces of dry pasta are usually used when making minestrone, but I wanted to turn this into more of a main course by adding tortellini pasta instead. You can use any filling, whether it's meaty, cheesy or a veg one.

---

2 tbsp olive oil
1 onion, chopped
2 sticks celery, thinly sliced
1 tbsp tomato purée
1 tsp paprika
2 cloves garlic, crushed
1 large carrot, grated
1 courgette (zucchini), finely chopped
1 litre/1¾ pints/scant 4¼ cups vegetable
   stock
1 x 400g/14 oz tin chopped tomatoes
handful or two of seasonal greens, finely
   shredded, such as cabbage, kale, chard
   or spinach
250g/9 oz packet of fresh tortellini, filling
   of your choice
flaked sea salt and freshly ground
   black pepper

To serve
1 tbsp pesto, mixed with 2 tbsp olive oil
Parmesan shavings or grated

Time taken 40 minutes / **Serves** 4–6

Heat the olive oil in a large saucepan over a low-medium heat and add the onion and celery. Sauté for about 8–10 minutes until softened. Add the tomato purée and paprika. Stir around for 30 seconds or so until the onion and celery are a lovely brick red colour, then add the garlic, carrot and courgette. Continue to sauté for a couple of minutes to soften.

Stir in the stock, chopped tomatoes and season with salt and pepper. Bring to a simmer, cover with a lid and cook over a low heat for 10 minutes.

Stir in the greens of your choice and then add the tortellini. Return to a simmer and cook for 3–4 minutes, or for the time stated on the pasta packet.

Spoon the minestrone and tortellini into bowls, drizzle over some pesto sauce and finish with some Parmesan shavings.

Flexible

Traditional minestrone: *if you want to serve up a more traditional version of a minestrone soup, omit the tortellini and add 75g / 2¾ oz dried spaghetti, broken up into small pieces, to the pan with the stock and chopped tomatoes.*

Make it meaty: *for a more meaty option to tortellini, fry some ready prepared or homemade meatballs (beef, lamb, chicken, pork or turkey) in a frying pan until golden brown and stir into the minestrone pan when you add the stock and tomatoes. Cook as above.*

Roast tomato and lentil soup

with halloumi croutons

When it comes to soup-making this will definitely come under the low maintenance category. The only real effort required is chopping a few veggies and throwing them in a roasting tray and letting the oven do all the work. However, to turn this into a super-charged soup, I like to add some red split lentils. The end result is a satisfying, heart-warming soup full of nutritional goodness. And if that's not enough, then there's the amazing halloumi croutons too.

For the soup

850g/1 lb 14 oz ripe tomatoes, quartered and green core removed

1 red (bell) pepper, quartered and deseeded

3 carrots, quartered

2 sticks celery, halved

1 long red chilli, halved (optional)

4 cloves garlic, peeled

3 tbsp olive oil

2 tsp paprika

100g/3½ oz red split lentils

1 litre/1¾ pints/scant 4¼ cups hot vegetable stock

flaked sea salt and freshly ground black pepper

basil leaves, to garnish

For the croutons

olive oil

200g/7 oz halloumi, diced into small cubes

Time taken 1 hour 10 minutes / **Serves** 6

Preheat the oven to 200°C/180°C fan/400°F/gas 6.

Put the tomatoes, pepper, carrots, celery, chilli, if using, and garlic in a large roasting tray, one that is suitable to be put on the hob as well as the oven. Drizzle with the olive oil, sprinkle over the paprika and season with salt and pepper. Toss to coat the veggies in the oil and roast in the oven for about 40 minutes, turning once or twice, until the vegetables are all softened and beginning to char nicely around the edges.

Remove the tray from the oven and stir in the lentils and stock. Place the roasting tray on the hob and set over a high heat. Bring to a simmer. Cover with foil or a baking sheet, reduce to a low-medium heat and cook for 15 minutes until the lentils are tender.

Blend the soup with a hand blender or liquidiser until smooth. If using a liquidiser, it may need to be done in two batches, depending on the size of your machine. Check for seasoning and serve hot.

To make the croutons, heat a drizzle of olive oil in a non-stick frying pan. Add the halloumi and fry for 2–3 minutes, turning throughout, until golden on most sides. Serve hot scattered on top of the soup along with the basil leaves.

Flexible

Vegan: *the soup itself won't need any alterations to be vegan friendly, but as an alternative to the halloumi croutons, lightly fry a mixture of cashew nuts and pumpkin seeds in a drizzle of oil until golden. Sprinkle over a pinch of smoked paprika and salt. Toss to coat and serve scattered on top of the soup.*

Dairy-free: *for dairy-free meat eaters, replace the halloumi by frying some sliced chorizo in a drizzle of oil until golden. Sprinkle over the soup with a drizzle of the rich red chorizo oil from the frying pan.*

Chilled watermelon gazpacho

This light and refreshing gazpacho is a perfect blend of sweet and savoury, making it very appealing for people of all ages, especially kids. My two have become big fans, especially when they can dunk some oily focaccia or ciabatta bread in to soak up the soup.

It's quick to make, as there's no cooking, everything just gets blended together and served cold. It can be prepared ahead of time too, then kept chilled in the fridge for 2–3 days.

600g/1 lb 5 oz watermelon flesh
   (from about 1kg/2 lb 4 oz wedge of
   watermelon), cut into chunks and
   seeds removed
½ cucumber, roughly chopped
3 ripe medium-size tomatoes, roughly
   chopped
1 red (bell) pepper, deseeded and
   roughly chopped
4 spring onions (scallions), roughly
   chopped
50ml/1¾ fl oz rapeseed (canola) or
   olive oil, plus extra for drizzling
1 tbsp red wine vinegar
flaked sea salt and freshly ground
   black pepper

To serve (optional)
finely diced watermelon, cucumber
   and tomato
basil or mint leaves
pumpkin seeds, lightly toasted

Time taken 15 minutes + 30 minutes chilling / **Serves** 6

Put all the gazpacho ingredients in a blender or liquidiser, add a good pinch of salt and twist of pepper. Blitz well until completely smooth. Chill for around 30 minutes.

Spoon into bowls, glasses or cups and enjoy as it is or scatter with diced watermelon, cucumber and tomato, basil or mint leaves and toasted pumpkin seeds. Add a drizzle of olive oil to serve.

Flexible

Traditional gazpacho: for a more traditional tomato gazpacho, omit the watermelon and increase the quantity of tomatoes to weigh 1kg/2 lb 4 oz, making sure they are really ripe. Remove their seeds and blend with all the other ingredients, plus the addition of 1 garlic clove and a pinch of dried chilli flakes. If you have sherry vinegar, then use it instead of red wine vinegar. Blend until smooth and serve with a drizzle of olive oil, twist of black pepper and finely diced cucumber and red (bell) pepper.

Leftover watermelon: if you've bought a large watermelon for the soup then why not use the leftover fruit to make the Tropical Ice Pops on page 172. Or you can blend to a liquid and serve as a chilled juice drink with the addition of fresh lime juice and coconut water for the kids, and a decent sized splash of citrus or plain vodka for the grown-ups!

Simple pho

Pho is a Vietnamese soup consisting of
broth, noodles and a variety of toppings.
It's proper feel-good food leaving you full
and satisfied, yet revived and refreshed.
This is a very simplified version that is
do-able midweek, and ideal for those
in-and-out days. Once you have the
aromatic broth made, you can heat up
individual portions when required, then
finish it off in the bowls with seasonings,
noodles and your chosen toppings.

For the broth

½ tsp dried chilli flakes

8 cloves

2 star anise

1 tsp coriander seeds

1 cinnamon stick

1.5 litres/2¾ pints/6¼ cups chicken or
vegetable stock

5cm/2 inch piece ginger, peeled and sliced

2 cloves garlic, halved

soy sauce, fish sauce or flaked sea salt,
to taste

juice of 1 lime

To finish

about 250–350g/9–12 oz cooked chicken,
pork or beef, or prawns (raw or cooked)

200g/7 oz vegetable selection, such as
baby corn, sugar snap peas, tenderstem
broccoli, mange tout, all halved or
quartered

2 pak choi, stalk sliced and leaves left
whole

250g/9 oz flat rice noodles

4 spring onions (scallions), finely sliced

100g/3½ oz beansprouts

1 red or green chilli, finely sliced

small bunch of mint or coriander (cilantro),
broken into sprigs

Time taken 45 minutes / **Serves** 4

To make the broth, heat a large pan or wok over a medium-high
heat. Add the chilli flakes, cloves, star anise, coriander seeds and
cinnamon stick. Toss around in the pan for 30 seconds or so to
lightly toast and release their aroma. Add the stock, ginger and
garlic, being careful as the liquid may spit. Bring to the simmer,
cover with a lid and cook for 20–30 minutes.

Strain the stock through a sieve, which will now be wonderfully
aromatic, and discard the spices. Return the stock back to the
pan and put over a medium heat. Season to taste with soy sauce,
fish sauce, tamari or salt and the lime juice. Return to a simmer.

If you're using cooked meat as your protein, very thinly slice or
shred it. The prawns can be left whole. Add to the pan along with
your chosen vegetables and sliced pak choi stalks. Return to a
simmer and cook for 3–4 minutes. If you're using raw prawns
make sure they are pink and cooked through, simmering for
longer if needed.

Meanwhile, cook the noodles according to the packet
instructions. Drain and divide between deep bowls.

To serve, spoon the broth, meat or prawns and vegetables on
top of the hot noodles. Add the pak choi leaves, spring onion,
beansprouts, chilli and herbs. Serve straight away.

Flexible

Gluten-free: make sure you use tamari rather than soy sauce.

*Vegetarian/vegan: make the broth using vegetable stock and use soy sauce
or salt in the place of fish sauce. A simple alternative to the meat or prawns
is to add some sliced shiitake mushrooms and/or diced tofu to the broth.
For a richer flavour, you can make some crispy baked tofu. To do this you
will need to cut 250g/9 oz extra-firm tofu into bite-size cubes, and dry with
plenty of kitchen paper, pressing out as much liquid as you can. Toss the
cubes in 1 tablespoon sunflower oil and 1 tablespoon soy sauce. Scatter with
1 tablespoon cornflour and toss again. Spread onto a baking sheet and
bake at 200°C/180°C fan/400°F/gas 6 for 20–25 minutes until golden,
tossing half way through. Serve scattered on top of your finished Pho.*

Cauliflower and chickpea soup

I've taken the basic flavours used to make the much-loved hummus into a soup along with oh-so-trendy cauliflower (who knew cauliflower had so many uses?). The end result is a very well-balanced, creamy soup that tastes fantastic, and furthermore, it's totally suitable for numerous dietary requirements. Simplicity at its best.

---

1 large cauliflower, cut into bite-sized florets and the stalk into chunks

6 cloves garlic, peeled

1 tsp cumin seeds

½ tsp ground coriander

5 tbsp olive oil

1 x 400g/14 oz tin chickpeas, drained

250g/9 oz white potatoes, peeled and diced

1.3 litres/2¼ pints/5½ cups vegetable stock

3 tbsp tahini

flaked sea salt and freshly ground black pepper

crusty bread, to serve

Time taken 1 hour / **Serves** 4–6

Heat the oven to 180°C/160°C fan/350°F/gas 4.

Put the cauliflower florets in a roasting tray. Add the garlic, cumin, coriander and 4 tablespoons of the olive oil. Season with salt and pepper and toss together until the cauliflower is coated in the spices. Roast in the oven for 40 minutes turning every so often until the cauliflower is tender and becoming golden.

Meanwhile, heat the remaining olive oil in a saucepan. Add the chickpeas, potatoes and cauliflower stalk. Fry for a couple of minutes and then add the stock. Bring to a simmer, cover with a lid and cook for about 12–15 minutes until the cauliflower and potatoes are tender.

Once the cauliflower florets are roasted, add to the saucepan along with the tahini. Use a handheld blender to blitz to a smooth consistency. Alternatively, you can do this in a free-standing blender or liquidiser though you may need to do this in a couple of batches, depending on the capacity of your blender.

Check for seasoning and serve the soup hot with crusty bread.

Flexible

Upgrade: *serve the soup with some spiced roasted chickpeas. To do this, drain 1 x 400g / 14 oz tin of chickpeas. Dry with kitchen paper and put on a baking tray. Toss with 2 teaspoons garam masala, ½ teaspoon dried chilli flakes, 1 teaspoon flaked sea salt and 3 tablespoons olive oil. Roast in the oven at the same time as the cauliflower for 40 minutes, shaking the tray every so often until the chickpeas are golden and crunchy. Cool and serve scattered on top of the soup and enjoy any leftovers to snack on over the next few days.*

Mexican street corn and prawn chowder

This creamy corn soup is mildly spiced and would be delicious eaten just as it is. However, I highly recommend finishing it off with the golden tinged prawns and sweetcorn kernels, which have been quickly pan-fried with lime juice to give them a bittersweet zing.

If you want to plan ahead with this one, make the chowder and heat up when required. Serve with crunchy tortilla chips, either shop bought or try making your own.

---

3 tbsp olive oil

25g/1 oz butter

1 onion, finely chopped

1 stick celery, finely chopped

1 green chilli, deseeded (or leave in for added spice) and chopped

2 cloves garlic, grated or crushed

1½ tsp ground cumin

3 tbsp plain (all-purpose) flour

1 litre/1¾ pints/scant 4¼ cups chicken or vegetable stock

350g/12 oz sweetcorn

200g/7 oz raw king prawns

1 lime

4 tbsp single (light) cream

small bunch coriander (cilantro), roughly chopped

flaked sea salt and freshly ground black pepper

tortilla chips, to serve (shop-bought or see the flexible tip)

Time taken 30 minutes / **Serves** 4

Place a medium-large saucepan over a medium heat and add 2 tablespoons of the olive oil and the butter. Once the butter has melted, stir in the onion and celery. Cook for about 5 minutes to soften the vegetables, before adding the chilli and garlic. Cook for a further few minutes and then add the cumin and flour.

Cook the flour for about 30 seconds or so by mixing around in the pan, then add the stock, stirring well to blend in any lumps of flour. Add three-quarters of the sweetcorn and season with salt and pepper. Bring to a simmer and cook gently for 10 minutes.

Meanwhile, pat the prawns dry with kitchen paper and season with a pinch of salt. Heat a large frying pan over a high heat and add the remaining olive oil. Add the prawns and fry until they are pink and turning golden. Squeeze in the juice of half a lime, which will instantly sizzle and give golden tinges to the prawns. Finally, add the remaining sweetcorn, tossing the pan over a high heat to take on a bit of colour.

Stir the cream and coriander into the soup, reserving some coriander for garnish, and check for seasoning, adding extra if needed. Ladle into bowls, spoon the prawns and corn on top and scatter with coriander. Serve straightaway with some tortilla chips to dip in and the remaining lime cut into wedges.

Flexible

Gluten-free: *be sure to use gluten-free flour in the chowder.*

Dairy-free: *swap the butter for coconut oil and use coconut cream or a dairy-free alternative to single (light) cream.*

Vegetarian: *simply swap the prawns for some diced feta cheese and / or diced avocado. Fry the feta in a hot pan as you would the prawns to give it some colour and serve on top of the soup.*

Tortilla dippers: *brush both sides of flour or corn tortilla wraps (gluten-free if necessary) with olive oil and cut into triangle shapes. Lay in a single layer on a baking sheet. Sprinkle with flaked sea salt and spices, such as smoked paprika, cayenne pepper, ground cumin or coriander. Bake for about 6–7 minutes in the oven set at 200°C / 180°C fan / 400°F / gas 6 until golden and crisp.*

Creamy pea, spinach and cashew soup

We actually just call this 'pea soup' in our house as the kids weren't keen on knowing there was spinach and cashew nuts in it, so I shortened its title to reduce the moaning. However, without these the soup wouldn't have its wonderful vibrant colour and creaminess, not to mention the punch of nutritional goodness. The kids know no different and enjoy it anyway, so it's a winner all round.

125g/4½ oz cashew nuts
2 tbsp or olive oil
1 large onion, chopped
1 stick celery, finely chopped
700ml/1¼ pints/scant 3 cups
   hot vegetable stock
500g/1 lb 2 oz frozen peas
100g/3½ oz fresh spinach
flaked sea salt and freshly ground
   black pepper
crusty bread, to serve

Time taken 30 minutes / **Serves** 4–6

Put the cashew nuts in a bowl and pour over enough boiling water to thoroughly cover. Set aside to soften.

Meanwhile, heat the oil in a large saucepan over a medium heat. Add the onion and celery, and gently sauté for about 10–12 minutes until they are softened but not coloured.

Increase the heat and pour in the stock. Bring the stock to the boil and then stir in the peas and spinach. Once the stock returns to the boil, cook for 1 minute, then remove from the heat.

Drain the cashews and transfer them to a blender or food processor with 200ml/7 fl oz/scant 1 cup cold water. Blitz thoroughly until you have a really smooth and creamy consistency. Reserve about one-quarter of the cashew cream for spooning on top of the soup when serving and keep the rest in the blender.

Ladle the soup into the blender with the cashew cream and blitz until smooth – work in batches if necessary.

Return the soup to the pan, season with salt and pepper to taste and reheat if needed. Spoon into bowls and dollop on or swirl in the reserved cashew cream and serve with crusty bread.

Flexible

Nut-free: *the cashew nuts can be substituted for 125g / 4½ oz silken tofu, which blends really nicely into the soup and also gives you a low-fat, high-protein addition, too.*

Get ahead: *as with most soups, I'll often make this in a big batch and freeze half in individual portions for an emergency nutritious lunch.*

Roast chicken broth... and 3 ways to use it

Making a broth or stock out of the leftover bones from a roast chicken is definitely a great way of making the most of your meat. I'm not suggesting anything ground-breaking here but I wanted to remind you how easy it is and how versatile the results can be.

For the broth

1 leftover roast chicken carcass, the bigger the better

2 onions, unpeeled and halved

8 cloves garlic, peeled and halved

3 carrots, roughly chopped

2 sticks celery, roughly chopped

3 bay leaves

½–1 tsp black peppercorns

2–3 sprigs fresh thyme

flaked sea salt

Time taken 2 hours / **Makes** about 3 litres/ 5¼ pints/just over 3 quarts

Put the chicken bones and any skin or bits you'd usually throw out into a very large pan. Cover with just enough cold water to submerge them. Add the remaining ingredients and bring to a simmer. Leave the pan uncovered and simmer for 1½–2 hours. You can always simmer this in a low oven, 120°C/100°C fan/250°F/ gas ½ if you'd prefer.

Once it's ready, strain the broth through a sieve into another large pan or heatproof containers, being careful as you do as it can splash. I find sitting the containers in the sink is an easier option. Throw away the chicken bones, vegetables and aromatics, or you can always keep back the carrot, onion and celery. They are very well cooked but melt-in-the-mouth delicious to eat straight away with a sprinkle of salt!

The broth can now be seasoned with salt and used straightaway, left to cool and stored in the fridge for up to 1 week, or frozen in smaller quantities.

Chicken noodle and vegetable broth

This is a firm favourite in my house. Heat up around 1.2 litres/2 pints/5 cups broth in a large pan. Add 1 finely chopped carrot and celery stalk. Simmer for a few minutes until tender before adding 2 large handfuls of mixed vegetables, cut into small pieces where necessary, such as green beans, broccoli, peas, sweetcorn or courgette (zucchini). Also throw in about 300g/10½ oz leftover roast chicken and a couple of strips or nests of dried egg noodles. Simmer until the noodles are tender and the veggies just cooked. Stir through some soy sauce and serve with optional chilli sauce to drizzle over the top or dried chilli flakes to scatter over.

Green noodle and sausage broth

If we've run out of leftover roast chicken this is what we'll have with the broth. Remove the skin from 4 chunky sausages and add to the pan. Break into smaller pieces and cook on a high heat until golden. Add 1.2 litres/2 pints/5 cups broth to a large pan, bring to the boil and stir in 150g/5½ oz dried spaghetti, broken into pieces. Simmer until the pasta is almost cooked, adding 2 large handfuls of small broccoli florets and some peas for the last few minutes. When the broccoli is cooked, stir through 2 tablespoons green pesto and add a good grating of Parmesan cheese.

Chicken barley broth

Heat up around 1.2 litres/2 pints/5 cups broth in a large pan. Add about 300g/10½ oz shredded leftover roast chicken, 250g/9 oz ready-to-eat barley (spelt, freekeh or other pre-cooked grain can also be used) and 200g/7 oz green beans. Simmer until the beans are tender. Stir in 25g/1 oz butter, grated zest of ½ lemon and ½ chopped red chilli.

snacks and small plates

Baked pea and paneer samosas

These are a huge hit in my house. The kids can't get enough of them. Luckily they're simple enough to make using everyday ingredients, so I'll often make them without any pre-planning as a welcomed surprise lunch or snack. I find they are a great tool for homework bribery!

Once cooked, the samosas can be served hot or cold, as a snack, starter, lunch with chutney and raita, or as an accompaniment to a curry feast.

----

2 tbsp sunflower or rapeseed (canola) oil,
   plus extra for brushing

1 small onion, finely chopped

1 carrot, grated

2 cloves garlic, crushed or grated

1 tsp fresh grated ginger

1 tbsp korma paste

1 tsp tomato purée

200g/7 oz paneer cheese, finely diced

2 tbsp desiccated coconut

175g/6 oz frozen peas, defrosted

4 sheets filo pastry

1–2 tsp nigella seeds and/or sesame
   seeds

flaked sea salt

mango chutney, to serve

Time taken 45 minutes / **Makes** 16

Heat the oil in a frying pan. Add the onion, carrot, garlic and ginger and sauté for about 10 minutes until the onion is beautifully soft.

Stir in the korma paste, tomato purée, paneer, coconut, peas, 1 tablespoon water and a pinch of salt. Cook for about 5 minutes, stirring frequently, until the filling has all cooked together nicely. Check for seasoning and add more salt if you feel it needs it. Remove the pan from the heat and cool slightly.

Preheat the oven to 200°C/180°C fan/400°F/gas 6.

Cut each piece of the filo pastry widthways into 4 strips, about 10cm/4 inches wide. Working on 4 strips at a time, brush each one lightly with oil. To prevent the remaining pastry from drying out, keep it covered with a damp tea towel.

Spoon a heaped tablespoon of the filling onto the bottom corner of each lightly oiled pastry strip. Fold over diagonally to create a triangle over the filling. Continue to fold/roll the pastry around the filling, keeping the triangle shape, securing in the filling. Once all 4 strips are filled and folded, place on a baking sheet. Continue with the remaining strips of pastry until you have used all the filling and pastry strips.

Brush the top of each samosa with a little oil and sprinkle over some nigella seeds and/or sesame seeds. Bake for 15–18 minutes until the pastry is golden and crisp. Once cooked, leave to cool for a few minutes before eating warm with the chutney, or leave to cool completely and enjoy cold.

Flexible

Vegan/dairy-free: *the equivalent weight of drained, tinned chickpeas are a tasty and suitable alternative to the paneer cheese.*

Pescatarian: *roughly chop 200g/7 oz cooked North Atlantic prawns and use in the place of the paneer cheese.*

Meat-lovers: *cook 200g/7 oz lamb, beef or chicken mince in with the sautéed onion mixture until cooked through and use in place of the paneer cheese.*

Danish crackers

with tuna spread and pickled cucumber

I should warn you now – these crackers are very hard to stop nibbling on. However, the warning comes with a positive note as they are so good for you it really shouldn't matter as they are packed full of nutrient-rich seeds and healthy oils. Aside from eating on their own, they make a great starter or lunchtime snack served with this family friendly creamy tuna spread and tangy pickled cucumber.

For the crackers (wheat-free)

150g/5½ oz rye flour

50g/1¾ oz pumpkin seeds

25g/1 oz porridge oats

25g/1 oz sunflower seeds

25g/1 oz sesame seeds

25g/1 oz flaxseeds

1½ tsp baking powder

1 tsp flaked sea salt

5 tbsp olive or rapeseed (canola) oil

For the pickled cucumber

6 mini cucumbers or ½ cucumber, thinly sliced

2 tbsp white wine vinegar

2 tsp caster (superfine) sugar

1 tsp flaked sea salt

For the tuna spread

200g/7 oz tinned tuna, in oil, brine or water, drained

125g/4½ oz cream cheese

50g/1¾ oz Greek yoghurt

1 tsp hot horseradish sauce

squeeze of lemon juice

flaked sea salt and freshly ground black pepper

Time taken 1 hour / **Makes** 4–8 portions, depending on whether you are serving this as a snack or lunch

Preheat the oven to 180°C/160°C fan/350°F/gas 4.

Place all the ingredients for the crackers in a bowl with 5 tablespoons water and mix together to form a wet dough.

Divide the dough in half and, working with one half at a time, sandwich between 2 large sheets of baking parchment. Use a rolling pin to roll the dough as thinly as you can. Remove the top sheet of paper and slide the bottom piece onto a baking sheet. Repeat with the remaining half of dough, sliding it onto a separate baking sheet. Bake for 20–25 minutes until golden and crisp.

Meanwhile, to prepare the cucumbers, simply mix everything together and leave for at least 15 minutes, stirring a couple of times.

To make the tuna spread, put everything in a bowl along with a pinch of salt and pepper, and mix well to form a paste consistency. Have a taste and add any extra lemon, horseradish or seasoning if it needs it.

Break the crackers into shards as big or small as you like and serve with the tuna spread and pickled cucumber.

Flexible

Dairy-free: switch the cream cheese and Greek yoghurt for dairy-free alternatives.

Upgrade: tuna is fairly mild in flavour, so a very family friendly fish for this type of recipe. However, if you wanted to go a little more 'grown-up' on the spread, then use the same weight in hot smoked salmon or smoked mackerel. Mix with the above ingredients along with some capers and chopped dill, and perhaps call it a 'pâté' rather than 'spread'.

Popcorn cauliflower bites

Dipping anything in breadcrumbs and frying until golden is always going to be a winner, and for anyone telling you they don't like cauliflower, they may well change their minds if they try this.

They're a brilliant party food snack, or a starter when entertaining. To avoid last-minute rushing around, coat the cauliflower florets in the crumbs and keep chilled, in a single layer on a tray. Then all you need to do is fry them and serve with garlic mayonnaise, ketchup, chilli mayonnaise or just a squeeze of lemon.

200g/7 oz chickpea (gram) flour
   or plain (all-purpose) flour
1 tsp smoked paprika
1 tsp dried oregano
1 tsp garlic salt
350ml/9 fl oz/1½ cups milk of choice
1 cauliflower, broken into bize-size florets
150g/7 oz panko breadcrumbs
sunflower oil, for frying
garlic mayonnaise, to serve

Time taken 30 minutes / **Serves** 8 as a snack

Whisk the flour, paprika, oregano, garlic salt and milk together until you have a smooth batter.

Dip the cauliflower florets in the batter, allowing excess to drip off and then roll them in the breadcrumbs to evenly coat.

Fill a wok or deep frying pan with about 5cm/2 inches sunflower oil and place over a medium-high heat. When the oil is shimmering, working in a few batches, carefully add the cauliflower florets. They should start to instantly sizzle when hitting the hot oil. Fry for about 2–3 minutes until nicely golden and crisp.

Remove with a slotted spoon and drain on kitchen paper. Repeat with the remaining cauliflower florets.

Serve with the garlic mayonnaise to dip into.

Flexible

Gluten-free: *use gluten-free breadcrumbs if you can get them; alternatively swap the crumbs for polenta or fine cornmeal.*

Upgrade: *you don't have to stick to a garlic mayonnaise to serve with the cauliflower fritters. You can try all sorts of dipping options, shop-bought or homemade. Combining equal quantities of a creamy blue cheese, such as dolcelatte, with sour cream or crème fraiche and a handful of snipped chives is a favourite of mine, or mayonnaise mixed with chipotle and lime juice is a close second.*

Mediterranean baked peppers

This is a go-to recipe, mainly for the warmer months as a light lunch, starter or even as a side dish to a roast chicken or some fish. As the peppers are roasted they become soft and juicy and their natural sweetness becomes more intense. You can be very flexible with your filling depending on what you've got already or what favours everyone fancies. I quite like to set up a pick 'n' mix station and get people to fill their own before baking.

---

4 (bell) peppers of your choice

3 tbsp pesto, tapenade or sun-dried tomato paste

2 ripe tomatoes, quartered, or 8 cherry tomatoes, halved

1 small red onion, finely sliced

small handful of fresh basil, parsley or oregano

1 tbsp balsamic vinegar

extra virgin olive oil

flaked sea salt and freshly ground black pepper

Optional fillings

pitted olives

capers

pine nuts

chopped artichokes (in oil from the jar)

anchovies or flaked tuna in oil

thinly sliced cured meats, such as Parma ham, Serrano ham, chorizo, salami

cheeses, such as mozzarella, brie, goat's cheese, Parmesan, feta, halloumi, dolcelatte

Time taken 50–60 minutes / **Serves** 4

Preheat the oven to 200°C/180°C fan/400°F/gas 6.

Cut the peppers in half lengthways, keeping the stalk intact if possible, as they look nicer that way when cooked. Remove the core, seeds and white membrane.

Spread the pesto, tapenade or sun-dried tomato paste inside each halved pepper and add the tomatoes, onion and fresh herbs.

Continue adding your chosen fillings, making sure you don't fill them too much otherwise they will stew rather than bake in the oven. Finish by drizzling with some balsamic vinegar, a decent glug of olive oil and season with salt and pepper.

Place the peppers on a baking tray and bake for 30–40 minutes until the peppers are softened but still just hold their shape and the fillings are melted, bubbling and slightly golden. Serve hot or warm and if you happen to have any leftovers they are just as delicious served cold.

Flexible

Plan-ahead: *once filled, the peppers can be put in the fridge and baked a few hours later. Drizzle with balsamic and oil just before baking.*

Baking on the barbecue: *sit the filled peppers in a heavy-based roasting tray, not one of your best / new ones though, and sit on the grill rack. Cook over medium temperature coals (at around 180–200°C / 350–400°F), with the lid on for around 30 minutes. This is ideal if you have a barbecue of which you are able to control the temperature to ensure you don't burn the base of the peppers. If you're not sure of the temperature just check the bottom of the peppers are not burning every now and again.*

Simple bao buns

with hoisin aubergine and quick pickled carrot

Time taken 50 minutes / **Serves** 8

*Chinese bao buns (pronounced 'bow')
are slightly sweet, steamed fluffy dough
pockets filled with a savoury treat.
Traditionally the buns are made using
yeast in the dough, which requires
kneading and rising before steaming.
Since most of us are time poor, I've
put together a quicker 'cheats' version.
As the dough has a sweetness to it,
the filling benefits from a powerful
punch of flavour provided by the
sticky hoisin aubergine.*

For the pickled carrot

3 tbsp white wine vinegar

1 tbsp caster (superfine) sugar

1 large carrot, peeled and cut into
matchsticks

For the buns

200g/7 oz self-raising (self-rising) flour,
plus extra for dusting

1 tbsp honey or agave syrup

1 tsp flaked sea salt

sunflower or rapeseed (canola) oil, for
brushing

For the filling

1 tbsp sunflower or rapeseed (canola) oil

1 tsp sesame oil

1 large aubergine (eggplant), cut into
1cm/½ inch dice

5 spring onions (scallions), thickly sliced

3 tbsp hoisin sauce

1 tsp toasted sesame seeds, to serve

First of all, pickle the carrot. Put the vinegar and sugar in a small saucepan and bring to the boil, stirring so the sugar dissolves. Remove from the heat and pour over the carrot. Mix well and set aside for the carrot to 'pickle'.

To make the bao buns, mix the flour, honey or agave syrup, salt and 100ml/3½ fl oz/scant ½ cup cold water until it forms a soft pliable dough. Dust the worktop with a little flour and knead the dough for a few minutes until it becomes smooth. Divide equally into 8 pieces and roll each one out to form an oval shape about 10 x 5cm/4½ x 2 inches. Brush the surface lightly with oil and fold in half. Continue with the remaining dough.

Set up a steamer to cook the buns. If you have a bamboo one, that is great as the excess moisture gets absorbed into the wood. If you are using a metal steamer on top of a pan, put a piece of baking parchment in the base of the steamer and wrap the lid in a clean tea towel to absorb excess moisture and prevent the buns becoming soggy. Sit the buns slightly apart from one another in the steamer. Cover with a lid and steam for 10 minutes until puffed up and bouncy when lightly pressed.

Meanwhile, make the filling. Heat the oils in a frying pan. Add the aubergine and toss around until golden and tender, adding a splash of water if it starts to burn. Add the spring onions and fry for a minute or so before adding the hoisin sauce and 2 tablespoons water. Cook for a couple of minutes until the sauce becomes thick and gives a sticky coating to the aubergine.

Once the bao buns are cooked, remove from the steamer, gently open up and fill with the sticky aubergine mixture and some pickled carrot. Scatter with sesame seeds and serve hot.

Flexible

Gluten-free: *use a gluten-free self-raising (self-rising) flour and add 1 teaspoon gluten-free baking powder. Mix to a smooth dough as per the recipe but there is no need to knead the dough for long due to the lack of gluten in the flour. Steam as above.*

Pescatarian: *fry some sliced spring onions (scallions) and grated ginger in sunflower oil, add 200g/7 oz raw prawns and toss until cooked. Flavour with some Szechuan, sweet and sour or hoisin sauce.*

Spiced chickpea fritters

with coriander yoghurt dip

These fluffy and mildly spiced fritters always go down well when served as part of an Indian-style sharing platter (with the Baked Pea and Paneer Samosas, see page 51) or as a starter before a curry, such as Mango and Coconut Chicken (see page 91) or Tikka Traybake (see page 115). However, because they are so straightforward to make, they're also really nice served with a tomato, cucumber, onion and coriander salad for lunch.

For the dip

200ml/7 fl oz coconut or Greek yoghurt
1 small bunch coriander (cilantro),
  finely chopped
pinch of flaked sea salt

For the fritters

1 x 400g/14 oz tin chickpeas, drained
4 spring onions (scallions), roughly
  chopped
1 green chilli, roughly chopped (keep in
  the seeds for a little more spice)
1 egg
4 tbsp chickpea (gram) flour
¼ tsp ground turmeric
1 tsp garam masala or mild curry powder
1 tsp flaked sea salt
sunflower oil, for frying
lime wedges, to serve

Time taken 30 minutes / **Serves** 6

First of all, make the dip by mixing together the yoghurt and coriander. Season with salt and set aside.

Put the chickpeas, spring onions, chilli, egg, flour, dried spices and sea salt in a blender or food processor and blend together until you have a thick batter.

Fill a wok or deep frying pan with about 5cm/2 inches sunflower oil and place over a medium-high heat. When the oil is shimmering, carefully drop spoonfuls of the fritter mixture into the hot oil and fry for 3–4 minutes until puffed up and lightly golden, turning with a slotted spoon halfway for even cooking. Remove with a slotted spoon and drain on kitchen paper while you continue using the remaining batter.

Serve the fritters hot with lime wedges and the dip on the side.

Flexible

Flavour swap: *for an equally as delicious but different flavoured fritter you can play around with the spices. Blend the chickpeas, egg, spring onions (scallions), green chilli and flour with 1 teaspoon harissa paste, ½ teaspoon ground cumin, ¼ teaspoon ground cinnamon and 1 teaspoon salt. Cook as above and serve with a dip made from 2 tablespoons tahini, 2 tablespoons water and 200ml/7 fl oz Greek yoghurt (dairy or plant-based), a squeeze of lemon juice and a small handful chopped mint or coriander (cilantro). Season to taste.*

Souvlaki pitta pockets
with tzatziki

Time taken 30 minutes + at least
30 minutes marinating / **Serves** 4–6

*Take yourselves off to the streets
of Greece and serve up this juicy
marinated chicken cooked either on a
griddle pan, or if the weather allows
outdoors, on a barbecue. Eat it the
authentic way, stuffed into warmed
pitta and topped with tzatziki. You can
throw in a few extras as well, such as
lettuce, tomatoes, olives or even some
hummus, for added goodness.*

For the souvlaki
400g/14 oz chicken breast or thigh
   fillets, skinless
1 tbsp dried oregano
1 tbsp dried mint
1 tsp paprika
2 cloves garlic, grated or crushed
juice of 1 lemon
75ml/2½ fl oz extra virgin olive oil
flaked sea salt

For the tzatziki
½ cucumber, coarsely grated
1 tsp flaked sea salt
1 small clove garlic, grated or crushed
1½ tsp red wine vinegar
2 tbsp finely chopped fresh mint or
   1 tsp dried mint
200g/7 oz Greek yoghurt

To serve
4–6 pitta bread, warmed
little gem lettuce
2 ripe tomatoes, sliced
kalamata olives, stoned
red onion, thinly sliced

Cut the chicken into 2cm/¾ inch chunks. Put in a bowl with the
rest of the souvlaki ingredients and add a good pinch of salt. Mix
everything together, cover and put into the fridge for 30 minutes, or
longer if you want the flavours to get a bit more intense. Overnight
would be absolutely fine.

To cook the souvlaki, the chicken will need skewers. Metal ones
are ideal, but if using wooden skewers, cut 8 to fit your griddle pan
and soak them in a tray of water for 30 minutes or so to stop them
burning during cooking.

To make the tzatziki, sit the cucumber in a sieve, mix in the salt
with your hands and squeeze out as much water as you can. Put
the cucumber in a bowl and mix with the garlic, vinegar, mint and
yoghurt. Season to taste and set aside.

Preheat a griddle pan or grill on a high heat. Thread the skewers
through the marinated chicken pieces, leaving little spaces between
them so that the heat cooks everything evenly. Cook the kebabs on
the hot griddle or grill for about 8–10 minutes, turning occasionally,
until deep golden on all sides.

Serve the souvlaki chicken stuffed inside warmed pitta bread with
some lettuce, tomato, olives and red onion. Top with dollops of
tzatziki and grab a napkin to wipe up any dripping juices.

Flexible

Gluten-free: *if you can replace the pitta bread with a gluten-free variety
or even some form of flat bread that's great. If not, lettuce leaves are a
simple alternative. Serve with some sautéed potatoes or chips on the side.*

Vegetarian: *halloumi is the perfect alternative to chicken.
Marinate as you would the chicken and grill for a few minutes,
turning occasionally, until golden.*

Meat-lovers: *don't just stick to chicken – pork fillet, lamb neck or turkey
breast are fantastic alternatives to marinate.*

Pescatarian: *if you're a seafood lover, try swapping the chicken for pieces
of squid or prawns. You'll only need to marinate them for around 30 minutes
and they will cook in minutes on a hot grill pan. Chunks of monkfish also
work very well as its meaty texture won't fall apart when cooking.*

Chicken noodle spring rolls

with soy dipping sauce

I don't make these any more... my kids make them instead! They've become really competitive as to who can make the fullest and neatest ones.

Depending on the size of the pastry sheets, you may end up with some trimmings left over. They can either be used for Baked Pea and Paneer Samosas (see page 51), or for a sweet treat, brush them with jam or chocolate and hazelnut spread, roll up into cigar shapes and bake for a few minutes until golden.

For the spring rolls
200g/7 oz cooked vermicelli rice noodles (using about 60g/2 oz dry noodles)
100g/3½ oz cooked chicken
100g/3½ oz carrot, grated
100g/3½ oz courgette (zucchini), grated
50g/1¾ oz edamame soy beans or peas (defrosted if frozen)
2 cloves garlic, grated
1 tsp grated ginger
1 tbsp soy sauce
1 tbsp sweet chilli sauce
12 sheets filo pastry
sunflower or rapeseed (canola) oil, for brushing
2 tsp sesame seeds

For the dipping sauce
2 tbsp soy sauce
1 tbsp rice or wine vinegar
1 tbsp honey

Time taken 45 minutes / **Makes** 6

Preheat the oven to 220°C/200°C fan/425°F/gas 7.

Place the vermicelli rice noodles in a mixing bowl and cut into slightly smaller pieces, using a pair of scissors.

Shred the chicken into thin strips using a fork or by tearing with your fingers and add to the noodles along with the carrot, courgette, edamame or peas, garlic, ginger, soy sauce and chilli sauce. Mix everything together.

Unroll the sheets of filo pastry onto the worktop and if they're not already, cut each into a square shape – different brands vary and some come as rectangular sheets.

To prevent the squares of pastry from drying out, cover with a tea towel. Re-wrap any trimmings and return to the fridge for use another day.

Lay 1 square of filo pastry on the surface and brush lightly with oil. Place another square of pastry on top and also brush with oil.

Turn the square so that one corner of the pastry is pointing towards you. Spoon one-sixth of the filling onto the corner nearest you. Fold this corner towards the centre and tuck under the filling.

Fold the two outside corners to the middle so it looks like an envelope. Brush the pastry lightly with oil then tightly roll it up, to look like a sausage shape.

please turn over

Brush once more and sit on a baking tray, with the join of the pastry underneath. Repeat until you have made all 6 spring rolls.

Scatter sesame seeds over the top of the spring rolls and bake for 15–18 minutes until they are lightly golden and crisp. Once cooked, leave to cool for around 10 minutes before eating as they will be piping hot inside.

To make the dipping sauce, put all the ingredients in a small bowl and mix together. Serve the spring rolls with the sauce to dip into.

Flexible

Vegetarian/vegan: *switch the chicken for the equivalent weight of firm or silken tofu, crumbled or broken into small pieces. You could also use agave or sugar instead of honey for a vegan dipping sauce.*

Pescatarian: *cooked North Atlantic prawns, tinned tuna or salmon are fantastic substitutes for the chicken.*

Gluten-free: *filo pastry is made with wheat flour, so you could use ready-made spring roll wrappers made with rice flour, though do check ingredients as many are made with wheat flour. An easier option would be to roll out ready-made gluten-free puff pastry as thin as you can, chill in the fridge for 30 minutes and then cut into 6 squares, using just one sheet per spring roll. The result isn't quite the same but tastes just as delicious.*

Quick pan pizza

OK, this may not be as quick as pizza delivery, but it's the fact that it's homemade which is important. The difference with this pizza as opposed to others, is that there's no waiting around for the dough to rise; it just goes straight into an ovenproof frying pan, topped with whatever you fancy, and baked. The heat from the outside of the pan acts like a heat blanket around the dough, making it light and airy as it cooks.

_____

For the dough

200g/7 oz plain (all-purpose) flour, white or wholemeal

7g packet/1½ tsp fast-action or easy blend dried yeast

1 tsp caster (superfine) sugar

½ tsp flaked sea salt

2 tbsp olive oil, plus extra for greasing

100ml/3½ fl oz warm water

For the topping

1–2 large spoonfuls of Flexible Tomato Sauce (see page 139) or 100ml/3½ fl oz passata or tinned chopped tomatoes

1 tsp dried oregano

1 small carrot, grated

½ courgette (zucchini), grated

2 cloves garlic, grated or crushed

1 tbsp olive oil, plus extra for drizzling

75g/2¾ oz mozzarella

flaked sea salt and freshly ground black pepper

Time taken 40 minutes / **Makes** 1 x approx. 23cm/9 inch pizza

Preheat the oven to 240°C/220°C fan/475°F/gas 9. Lightly oil a 23cm/9 inch ovenproof frying pan or loose-bottomed cake tin.

Put the flour, yeast, sugar, salt and olive oil in a bowl. Mix together, then stir in the water, bringing the mixture together to form a dough. Turn out onto the worktop and knead for a few minutes until smooth. Press the dough into the oiled tray, pushing into the edges as you go.

If you need to make the dough ahead of cooking it, press it into the pan and keep in the fridge until you are ready to add the toppings. I find this very handy when the kids are coming and going, needing feeding at different times.

Mix together the tomato sauce, passata, or tinned tomatoes, oregano, carrot, courgette, garlic and 1 tablespoon olive oil. Season with salt and pepper then spread over the dough leaving a small border around the edge.

Top with the mozzarella either grated or torn into small pieces. At this stage you can add more toppings should you wish. Drizzle with olive oil and bake for 20 minutes until the dough is golden around the edges.

Flexible

Gluten-free: simply swap the flour for a gluten-free flour and add 1 teaspoon xantham gum. Continue making the dough as per the recipe above.

Upgrade: as with any pizza, you can top it with as many ingredients and flavours as you wish such as olives, anchovies, chilli, fresh herbs, cheese, cured or cooked meats, prawns, vegetables etc.

Vietnamese pancakes

(Bánh Xèo)

These sunshine yellow coconut pancakes are naturally gluten- and dairy-free. Once you get the hang of making them they are very easy – it's often the first one or two that are never perfect, but that's the same for any pancake. The cook gets to eat those while cooking the rest! You need to keep the heat high to get the underside sizzling and crisp, before adding the filling and folding in half.

For the pancakes
300g/10½ oz rice flour
1 tbsp cornflour (cornstarch)
1 tsp ground turmeric
1 tsp flaked sea salt
200ml/7 fl oz tinned coconut milk
4 spring onions (scallions), very finely
  sliced
sunflower oil, for frying

For the filling
100g/3½ oz beansprouts
1 carrot or ¼ cucumber, cut into thin
  strips
2 handfuls cooked shredded chicken or
  pork (leftovers are great)
coriander (cilantro) and/or mint leaves

To serve
3 tbsp sweet chilli sauce
lime wedges

Time taken 30 minutes / **Serves** 4

To make the pancake batter, put the rice flour, cornflour, turmeric and salt in a mixing bowl. Give the coconut milk a good stir if it has separated and then add to the dry ingredients along with 200ml/7 fl oz/scant 1 cup water. Whisk with a balloon whisk to create a smooth thin batter, about the consistency of double (heavy) cream. Add any extra coconut milk or water if needed. Stir in the spring onions and set aside to rest for 10 minutes.

To cook the pancakes, heat a medium non-stick frying pan over a high heat and add a trickle of oil to lightly coat the surface. Once the pan is hot, add a ladle of the batter, swirling around the pan so it covers the base. The batter should sizzle and instantly create a lattice effect. Leave to cook for 1–2 minutes or so until the underside has become crisp and golden. Carefully lift the edge with a spatula to check.

While the pancake is cooking, scatter some beansprouts, carrot or cucumber, chicken or pork and some herbs over half the pancake. When the base of the pancake is lightly golden and crisp, carefully fold the pancake over the filling and slide onto a serving plate.

Repeat with the remaining batter and filling, adding a drop more oil into the pan each time. As the pan gets hotter you may want to reduce the heat slightly so the pancakes don't burn.

Serve straightaway with the sweet chilli sauce drizzled over the top, a squeeze of lime and extra sauce to dip into.

Flexible

Vegetarian/vegan: pan-fry some diced firm tofu in sunflower oil and season with soy sauce. Use as a filling in place of the chicken or pork.

Pescatarian: use cooked prawns instead of the chicken or pork in the filling. Serve cold or fry in a little oil to heat through before using to fill the pancakes.

Flavour swap: instead of sweet chilli sauce, serve with a classic Vietnamese dipping sauce, Nuoc Cham, made from combining 2 tablespoons light soy sauce or fish sauce with 2 tablespoons lime juice, 1 tablespoon palm or brown sugar, 1 grated garlic clove and 1 finely chopped red bird's-eye chilli.

Cheesy cornbread muffins

*After school, sport, activity or club…
the one thing most of us struggle
with is finding a suitable savoury
snack that's not packed with salt
and fat. It's so easy to grab a bag
of crisps or bought pastry, but with
a little pre-planning, this is where
these muffins work really well for
the kids and adults, too.*

*The muffins are also really
delicious served warm for brunch /
lunch, with some ham, eggs and / or
grilled tomatoes with some chipotle
mayonnaise on the side.*

150ml/5 fl oz/²⁄₃ cup milk

200ml/7 fl oz/scant 1 cup buttermilk

3 eggs

165g/5¾ oz sweetcorn (tinned is perfect)

3 spring onions (scallions), finely chopped

75ml/2½ fl oz rapeseed (canola) or
   olive oil

175g/6 oz fine polenta (cornmeal)

100g/3½ oz plain (all-purpose) flour

1 tbsp baking powder

50g/1¾ oz Cheddar cheese, grated

50g/1¾ oz feta cheese, crumbled

flaked sea salt

Time taken 40–45 minutes / **Makes** 12–18 muffins
(depending on the size you make)

Preheat the oven to 180°C/160°C fan/350°F/gas 4. Line a muffin
tin with baking parchment or silicone cases. Larger 'tulip' paper
cases will give you 12, but standard muffin cases will make up
to 18 cooked muffins.

Put the milk, buttermilk, eggs, sweetcorn, spring onions and oil
in a bowl and mix to combine.

In a separate bowl, mix together the polenta, flour, baking powder,
cheeses and a pinch of salt.

Pour the wet ingredients over the dried and mix briefly to just
combine. Avoid over-mixing as this will give you more dense
muffins when cooked.

Divide between muffin tins (for ease use an ice cream scoop).
Bake for 18–25 minutes, depending on their size, until they are
light golden brown and just firm to touch in the middle.

Cool in the tins for 10 minutes before cooling on a wire rack.
Serve warm or at room temperature. Eat within a couple of days,
and freeze any left over. Defrost at room temperature or warm
gently in the microwave or oven.

Flexible

Gluten-free: use gluten-free plain (all-purpose) flour and baking powder.

*Dairy-free: swap the milk for a dairy-free alternative such as oat, soya or
any nut milk. As a substitute for buttermilk, stir 1 tablespoon lemon juice
or white wine vinegar into your chosen dairy-free milk and leave it to sit
for about 10 minutes until it thickens and looks like it's curdled slightly.
Use in the recipe as above.*

*Both the Cheddar and feta cheese can be substituted for vegan / dairy-free
alternatives. It's amazing what's available in the shops when you look around.*

*Upgrade: 50g / 1¾ oz finely chopped ham, salami or chorizo can be mixed
into the mixture before baking. For a touch of spice, add a finely chopped
red or green chilli.*

main
meals

Slow-cooked Asian beef

I have fallen in love with this recipe. There is a little work involved in browning the meat and preparing the aromatics and spices, but once it's in the oven it looks after itself. You can carry on with your day, taking in the fantastic aroma, knowing it's getting better and better by the hour.

The flavour of the finished dish is rich, so best served with a plain rice and some simple steamed greens. Cucumber, Mango and Peanut Salad (see page 136) or Soy-Glazed Greens (see page 132) would also be a superb accompaniment.

———————————————

2 tbsp sunflower oil

1.3kg/3 lb beef shin or brisket, cut into large chunky pieces (2–3 per person)

1 tbsp sesame oil

2 onions, finely chopped

2 tbsp ginger, grated or finely chopped

4 cloves garlic, grated or crushed

1 red chilli, finely chopped

1 tsp coriander seeds, lightly crushed

2 star anise

1 cinnamon stick

400ml/14 fl oz/1⅔ cups beef stock

4 tbsp soy sauce

2 tbsp rice wine vinegar

4 tbsp soft brown sugar

1 tbsp Chinese 5-spice seasoning

To serve

1 red or green chilli, finely sliced

ginger, cut into matchsticks

3 spring onions (scallions), finely sliced

small bunch coriander (cilantro)

1 lime, cut into wedges

Steamed Basmati Rice (see page 124)

Time taken 5½ hours / **Serves** 4–6

Preheat the oven to 140°C/120°C fan/275°F/gas 1.

Heat a large casserole pan over a high heat with the sunflower oil. When hot, add the beef and brown well on all sides, working in batches if necessary. Remove the beef from the pan and set aside.

Add the sesame oil to the pan and then throw in the onions, ginger, garlic, chilli, coriander seeds, star anise and cinnamon to the pan and cook for about 5 minutes still over a high heat, until the onions are turning golden.

Stir in the beef stock, soy sauce, rice vinegar, sugar and Chinese 5-spice and bring up to a gentle simmer. Cover with a lid and cook in the oven for about 5 hours – though up to 6 hours is fine. If you need longer, then simply turn the oven down to 110°C/90°C fan/230°F/gas ¼.

When you are ready to serve, remove the pan from the oven. By now the beef will be so tender that it will start to fall apart. The sauce should be nicely rich and thickened a little. If you want a thicker consistency, carefully lift the meat out of the pan, put the sauce over a high heat and reduce to your preferred consistency.

Serve the meat either in pieces with the sauce spooned over, or tear the meat into strips in the sauce and serve with the chilli, ginger, spring onion, coriander and lime on top or on the side, and the steamed rice.

Flexible

Gluten-free: be sure to use tamari instead of soy sauce.

Flavour swap: the beef can be swapped for the same weight of pork shoulder (skin removed) and cooked in the same way. Tear the tender cooked pork into shreds and mix into the sauce at the end.

Upgrade: towards the end of the cooking time, you can throw in some water chestnuts and/or bamboo shoots.

Super veggie cottage pie

This is a delicious twist on a classic oven-baked comfort dish. It's packed full of nutritional goodness from numerous tasty veggies, beans, quinoa and lentils, and contains no meat at all. I've served this to many a meat eater who didn't miss, or even notice, the lack of meat at all! It may appear to be a lengthy list of ingredients but they are all wonderfully good for you, and the method is nice and simple, so don't be put off.

---

2 tbsp sunflower or rapeseed (canola) oil

1 large leek, finely chopped

2 carrots, grated

2 sticks celery, finely chopped

2 sprigs fresh rosemary

1 bay leaf

100g/3½ oz chestnut mushrooms, diced

3 tbsp tomato purée

2 tsp Worcestershire sauce (vegetarian if necessary)

1 x 400g/14 oz tin chopped tomatoes

500ml/17 fl oz/2 cups vegetable stock

200ml/7 fl oz/scant 1 cup red wine (or extra stock of preferred)

150g/5½ oz dried green lentils

150g/5½ oz quinoa

1 x 400g/14 oz tin haricot or cannellini beans, drained

flaked sea salt and freshly ground black pepper

For the topping

1.4kg/2 lb 4 oz mixed root vegetables (potatoes, parsnip and sweet potatoes – the quantity of each is up to you)

40g/1½ oz butter, plus extra for baking

3 tbsp milk

Time taken 1½ hours / **Serves** 6

Preheat the oven to 180°C/160°C fan/350°F/gas 4.

Heat the oil in a large saucepan and gently cook the leeks, carrot, celery, rosemary and bay leaf for 5 minutes. Add the mushrooms and continue to cook for a further 5 minutes or until all the vegetables are tender.

Stir in the tomato purée, Worcestershire sauce, chopped tomatoes, stock and wine. Bring to a simmer and stir in the lentils, quinoa and beans. Stir well and return to a simmer. Cover with a lid and cook for 30 minutes, stirring occasionally.

Meanwhile, cut the root vegetables into chunks, removing the tough core from the parsnip and cutting the potatoes slightly smaller than the other vegetables (they usually take a little longer to cook than the others). Place in a pan of boiling water and cook for about 10–15 minutes until tender. Drain and mash with the butter and milk and season with salt and pepper.

Place the pie filling in an ovenproof dish or individual dishes, top with the mash and dot some extra butter on top. Bake for 25–30 minutes until the tops are lightly golden and bubbling at the edges. If you are cooking from chilled, add a further 10 minutes to the cooking time.

Flexible

Vegan/dairy-free: *simply use a dairy-free butter and milk for the topping and make sure the Worcestershire sauce is vegan friendly.*

Flavour swap: *ring the changes and add a warmth of Moroccan spice to either the Super Veggie Cottage Pie or the classic lamb version. Omit the Worcestershire sauce and rosemary and replace with 1 teaspoon smoked paprika, 1 teaspoon ground cumin, ½ teaspoon ground cinnamon and 75g/2¾ oz raisins to the filling.*

Chicken and black bean tinga tacos

with watermelon salsa

This is super-easy to make and for that reason I serve it frequently at home. Tinga is a Mexican dish where chicken is cooked with onion, tomatoes and chipotle sauce and shredded when cooked. I like to do a half-half chicken and black bean combo, to vary things up and reduce our meat intake.

This juicy watermelon salsa is well worth making. Put everything on the table to make a sharing supper for everyone to dig into.

---

1 tbsp olive oil

1 onion, finely chopped

4 cloves garlic, grated or crushed

1 tsp dark brown sugar

1 tsp chipotle paste (or more for a spicier finish)

1 tsp red or white wine vinegar

400g/14 oz can chopped tomatoes

400g/14 oz can black beans or kidney beans, drained

2 chicken breasts, skinless or 350g/12 oz boneless chicken thighs

flaked sea salt and freshly ground black pepper

For the salsa

300g/10½ oz watermelon, diced into small pieces

4 spring onions (scallions), chopped

½ green chilli, deseeded and finely chopped

½ small bunch coriander (cilantro), chopped

juice of ½ lime

2 tbsp olive oil

To serve

1 large ripe avocado, sliced or mashed

sour cream

1 small red onion, finely sliced and mixed with juice of ½ lime

grated Cheddar cheese

coriander (cilantro) leaves, roughly chopped

soft corn or flour tortillas, warmed

Time taken 50 minutes / **Serves** 4

Heat the oil in a heavy-based saucepan or casserole dish. Add the onion and cook for 5 minutes or until softened and starting to turn golden. Add the garlic and cook for a further minute before stirring in the sugar, chipotle paste, vinegar, tomatoes, 200ml/7 fl oz/scant 1 cup water and the black beans. Mix everything together and bring to a simmer.

Add the chicken to the pan, spooning over the sauce to cover. Cover with a lid and simmer gently for 30 minutes until the chicken is cooked and the sauce thickened.

Meanwhile, make the salsa by mixing everything together in a serving bowl and seasoning with salt and pepper.

Once cooked, remove the chicken from the pan and sit on a plate or board. Using two forks, shred into strips and then return the shredded meat back to the sauce.

Serve the Chicken and Black Bean Tinga with the watermelon salsa, avocado, sour cream, red onion, cheese and coriander. Pile everything into warm tortillas, wrap and prepare to get messy.

Flexible

Pescatarian: *a delicious alternative to using chicken is to swap it for some chunky white fish such as cod, pollock or haddock. Let the tomato and black bean sauce cook alone for 20 minutes then add 400g / 14 oz fish fillets to the pan. Spoon over the sauce, cover with a lid and cook for 10 minutes. Break the fish into flakes in the pan and serve as above.*

Get ahead: *once made, the chicken can sit in the fridge for 3–4 days and heated through when needed. It can also easily be doubled up so you can freeze half for another time.*

Indian 'dosa' with spiced sweet potato

Authentic dosa pancakes are made by soaking, blending and fermenting black gram lentils (urad dal). Delicious as they are I wanted to make a recipe that can be made without too much advance thought and preparation. So, this is my take on dosa pancakes, which are wrapped around an aromatic spiced sweet potato and chickpea filling. I like to serve these with some mango chutney and coconut yoghurt mixed with chopped coriander and lime juice, or raita.

For the pancake batter

125g/4½ oz rice flour

125g/4½ oz chickpea (gram) flour

½ tsp bicarbonate of (baking) soda

2 tsp black mustard seeds

flaked sea salt

sunflower or rapeseed (canola) oil for cooking

Filling

500g/1 lb 2 oz sweet potatoes, peeled and cut into small chunks

2 tbsp sunflower or rapeseed (canola) oil

2 tsp fennel seeds

2 tsp cumin seeds

2 tsp coriander seeds

1 red chilli, deseeded for a milder flavour, finely chopped

1 large onion, finely sliced

25g ginger, peeled and finely chopped or grated

4 cloves garlic, peeled and crushed or grated

2 tbsp fresh or 1 tbsp dried curry leaves

1 tsp ground turmeric

1 x 400g/14 oz tin of chickpeas, drained and liquid reserved

small bunch coriander (cilantro), roughly chopped

chutneys and raita, to serve

Time taken 1 hour / **Serves** 4–6

To make the pancake batter, put the flours into a large bowl with the bicarbonate of soda, mustard seeds and a good pinch of salt. Gradually whisk in enough water, about 400ml/14 fl oz/1⅔ cups, to make a loose, smooth batter, like the consistency of double (heavy) cream. Set aside.

To make the filling, preheat the oven to 200°C/ 180°C fan/400°F/gas 6.

Toss the sweet potato in half the oil and spread out on a large baking tray. Bake for 20 minutes, stirring on the tray once or twice during cooking, until soft and starting to caramelise around the edges.

Meanwhile, heat the remaining oil in a large frying pan and fry the fennel, cumin and coriander seeds for around 30 seconds until they become fragrant. Stir in the chilli, onion, ginger, garlic, curry leaves and turmeric and cook over a low heat for 10 minutes until the onion is really soft, stirring occasionally.

Add the chickpeas and 100ml/3½ fl oz/scant ½ cup of the chickpea water. Stir well to bring all the flavours together.

Add the roasted sweet potato and chopped coriander to the pan and season with a good pinch of salt. Keep the mixture warm until the pancakes are ready.

please turn over

To cook the pancakes, heat 1 teaspoon oil in a large non-stick frying pan or pancake pan over a medium-high heat. Add a large spoonful of batter to the pan and immediately twist so the batter coats the base and slips up the edges.

As soon as the top of the pancake looks dry, starts to cook away from the sides of the pan and there are lots of bubbles, add a large spoonful of the sweet potato filling and gently spread across the dosa. Once the base is crispy, loosely roll up the dosa in the pan and transfer to a serving plate. Keep warm while you continue with the rest of the batter and filling. Serve with chutneys and raita.

Flexible

Root swap: *if you've some other root veggies to use up then you don't have to stick with sweet potatoes – white potatoes, swede, parsnip and butternut squash all work just as well in this recipe.*

Spice swap: *if the amount of individual spices in this recipe make your shopping list too long, then use any spices you have already – 1 tablespoon of a mild or medium curry powder could be used, alternatively 1–2 tablespoons curry paste is also fine.*

Sweet and sour pork meatball traybake

*Ordering sweet and sour in a Chinese
restaurant reminds me of my first
Chinese food experience as a child.
Now my own kids love the deep-fried
pieces of pork or chicken coated in
a sweet sticky sauce just as much as
I do, which is great, but only as an
occasional treat.*

*That's where this recipe comes in.
I wanted to make something we could
enjoy just as much but doesn't have
any guilt attached to it, and luckily
it gets a huge thumbs up from us all.*

For the meatballs

500g/1 lb 2 oz minced (ground) pork
60g/2 oz fresh white breadcrumbs
4 spring onions (scallions),
 finely chopped
2 cloves garlic, grated or crushed
2 tsp grated ginger
1 tsp Chinese 5-spice seasoning
1 egg, lightly beaten
flaked sea salt and freshly ground
 black pepper
2 tbsp sunflower or rapeseed
 (canola) oil

For the sauce

1 large onion, coarsely chopped
2 red, green, yellow or orange peppers,
 or 3 if they are small, cut into
 bite-size chunks
500ml/17 fl oz passata
250ml/9 fl oz/1 cup fresh pineapple juice
4 tbsp rice or cider vinegar
2 tbsp soy sauce
250g/9 oz pineapple, cut into chunks

Time taken 1 hour / **Serves** 4

Preheat the oven to 200°C/180°C fan/400°F/gas 6.

Mix together the minced pork, breadcrumbs, spring onions, garlic,
ginger, Chinese 5-spice, egg and season with salt and pepper. Shape
into walnut-sized balls.

Heat a heavy-based roasting tray over a high heat and add the oil.
Fry the meatballs for a few minutes, turning occasionally for an
even colour. They don't need to be fully cooked through at this stage,
just golden on the outside. Remove from the pan.

Reduce the heat to medium and add the onion and peppers to the
roasting tray, along with a drop more oil if necessary. Fry for a few
minutes until they start to take on some colour around the edges.
Stir in the passata, pineapple juice, vinegar and soy sauce and
bring to a simmer.

Return the meatballs to the sauce and add the pineapple. Gently
stir into the sauce and put the tray in the oven. Cook for 35 minutes
until the sauce is rich in colour and the vegetables are tender.

Flexible

*Vegetarian/vegan: Tofu and Shiitake 'Meatballs' are a perfect
alternative to the pork meatballs. Put 250g/9 oz extra-firm tofu,
100g/3½ oz shiitake mushrooms, 2 tablespoons milk (dairy
or plant-based) and 2 tablespoons ground flaxseed (as an egg
replacement) in a food processor with the above quantity of
breadcrumbs, spring onions (scallions), ginger, garlic, Chinese
5-spice and seasoning. Blitz well and firmly shape into walnut-
size balls. Fry until golden and add to the sauce for just the last
10 minutes of the oven cooking time.*

*Flavour swap: minced (ground) chicken, turkey or beef can be
used instead of pork.*

*Get ahead: the raw meatballs can be prepared ahead of time
and kept in the fridge for up to 2 days, or in the freezer for up to
3 months. Defrost in the fridge before cooking.*

Prawn laksa parcels

Time taken 35 minutes / **Serves** 4

Simple and quick to prepare, and exceptionally tasty when eaten. Cooking your whole meal in individual parcels is a great way of keeping in all the flavour and nutrients the ingredients provide. You can make these ahead of time and then cook individually when needed, or all together.

Malaysian Laksa paste is pretty easy to get hold of and is an aromatic blend of turmeric, ginger, lemongrass, galangal, to name just a few of its ingredients.

200g/7 oz raw flat rice noodles

500g/1 lb 2 oz stir-fry vegetables, such as mange tout, baby corn, tenderstem, sugar snap (thinly slice any of the thicker vegetables)

350g/12 oz raw peeled king prawns

150g/5½ oz beansprouts

4 tbsp laksa paste

400ml/14 fl oz coconut milk

175ml/6 fl oz/¾ cup fish stock

juice of ½ lime

4 tsp fish sauce

4 spring onions (scallions), finely sliced on the angle

small handful coriander (cilantro) leaves

lime wedges, to serve

Preheat the oven to 230°C/210°C fan/450°F/gas 8 and put a large baking tray in the oven to heat up.

Tear 4 large pieces of baking parchment and scrunch up to a tight ball. This helps make it more pliable. Open the paper out and sit each one in a bowl, making a well in the middle. As an alternative to baking parchment you can use foil, or you can even buy individual cellophane roasting bags, which work a treat.

Cook the rice noodles according to the pack instructions but if you can, try and leave them slightly undercooked/al dente. Drain and refresh under cold water. Divide between the 4 parcels.

Scatter the vegetables on top of the noodles along with the prawns and half the beansprouts.

Mix together the laksa paste, coconut milk, fish stock, lime juice and fish sauce and divide between the parcels.

Pull up the sides of each parcel and tie each one tightly with a piece of string. If you are using foil, scrunch together tightly, making sure you leave space in the top to allow steam to circulate. Give each bag a gentle mix/massage to make sure everything is coated in the laksa coconut stock.

Put the parcels on to the hot baking sheet and bake for 20 minutes, giving the bags a little shake half way through for even cooking.

Remove from the oven and split open each parcel into bowls. Scatter over the remaining beansprouts and the spring onions and coriander. Serve with lime wedges to squeeze over.

Flexible

Get ahead: the parcels can be prepared in advance and kept in the fridge for a good few hours before cooking.

Flavour swap: you can use other South-east Asian curry pastes in this recipe such as Thai red, green or yellow, penang, rendang, jungle, massaman, sambal oelek or nyonya.

Meat-lovers: a great swap for the prawns is to add thinly sliced cooked chicken.

Mango and coconut chicken

I started to make this recipe when the kids were little and I was trying to introduce more spice in their diet. The addition of mango brings a mellow sweetness to the curry, balancing out the spices perfectly.

For more heat, I like to scatter some chopped fresh chilli on mine at the end. Or for a hotter curry for everyone, you can add chilli flakes at the start. You can also cook veggies in the sauce to bulk it out.

---

2 tbsp coconut, sunflower or rapeseed (canola) oil
1 large onion, finely diced
2 tsp grated ginger
5 tbsp Korma or a mild curry paste
1 tbsp tomato purée
800g/1 lb 12 oz boneless chicken pieces (thigh or breast), cut into bite-size chunks.
1 x 400ml/14 fl oz tin coconut milk
1 large ripe mango, peeled and chopped into small pieces
75g/2¾ oz ground almonds
flaked sea salt

To serve
½ –1 mango, peeled and sliced
handful of toasted coconut flakes
Steamed Basmati Rice (see page 124)

Time taken 50 minutes / **Serves** 6

Heat the oil in a large wide saucepan over a medium-high heat. Add the onion and ginger. Sauté for about 8 minutes until the onion is softened and becoming golden.

Add the curry paste and tomato purée, stir for around 30 seconds or so before mixing in the chicken. Stir to coat in the paste and cook until the chicken has started to brown all over.

Mix in the coconut milk, mango and ground almonds. Bring to a simmer and cook uncovered for 30 minutes for the sauce to thicken and the chicken to cook through. Season to taste and serve with sliced mango, coconut flakes, and coriander on top alongside the basmati rice.

Flexible

Pescatarian: make the sauce as above but minus any chicken. Once its cooked, add skinless fillets of any sustainable white fish, salmon or even some prawns. Spoon over the sauce and bring to a simmer. They will only need 5–10 minutes cooking time, depending on their thickness.

Vegetarian: diced paneer, halloumi and chickpeas are good protein-rich substitutes for the chicken, with the addition of cauliflower florets and broccoli to bulk out the sauce.

Nut-free: if you can't have ground almonds then the same quantity of desiccated coconut can be used.

Moroccan baked fish in a bag

If you like the idea of very little washing-up, you're going to love this. It's a complete meal cooked all together in the oven, in individual parcels. The best thing to do is to prepare ahead and keep it in the fridge to cook later on in the evening. From a flexibility point of view, you can swap and change a few of the ingredients according to personal tastes too. Do make sure you label whose is whose though, to avoid any unwanted surprises!

---

2 x 400g/14 oz tin chopped tomatoes

1 x 400g/14 oz tin chickpeas, drained

small handful stoned black olives

handful dried apricots, chopped

1 carrot, grated

2 tsp harissa paste

2 roasted red (bell) peppers (from a jar), sliced or chopped

2 large handfuls baby spinach leaves

handful chopped coriander (cilantro)

4 fish fillets, such as cod, pollock, haddock or salmon

extra virgin olive oil, for drizzling

flaked sea salt and freshly ground black pepper

couscous or flatbreads, to serve

Time taken 30 minutes / **Serves** 4

Preheat the oven to 220°C/200°C fan/425°F/gas 7 and put a large baking tray in the oven to heat up.

Tear 4 large pieces of baking parchment and scrunch up to a tight ball. This helps make it more pliable. Open the paper out and sit each one in a bowl making a well in the middle. As an alternative to baking parchment you can use foil, or you can even buy individual cellophane roasting bags, which work a treat.

Divide the tomatoes between the parcels, then do the same with the chickpeas, olives, apricots, carrot, harissa, red pepper, spinach and coriander. Season and gently stir to mix.

Sit the fish fillets on top, season and drizzle with olive oil. Pull up the sides of each parcel and tie each one tightly with a piece of string. If you are using foil, scrunch together tightly, making sure you leave space in the top to allow steam to circulate.

The parcels can be prepared in advance and kept in the fridge for a good few hours before cooking at this stage.

Put the parcels on the hot baking tray and bake for 20 minutes until the fish is cooked through. When cooked, split open the parcels into bowls and serve hot with couscous or flatbreads.

Flexible

Flavour swap: if you fancy using some chicken for a change, add 1 small-ish chicken breast, cut into 4–5 slim pieces, to the bag and bake for 25 minutes.

Vegetarian: switching the fish for a 100–150g / 3½–5½ inch wedge of feta cheese is absolutely delicious and well worth a try.

Upgrade: make this look super-fancy by scattering over some chopped pistachios or flaked toasted almonds, chopped preserved lemons and fresh coriander (cilantro) sprigs too.

Mexican baked chicken and rice

This is an adaptation on a Mediterranean baked chicken and rice I've done many times in the past… probably too many as my family roll their eyes when I say we're having it for dinner, again! I have taken the same concept of cooking chicken, veg and rice in a tomatoey stock in the oven. I've altered the herbs and spices for a Mexican feel and am using wholegrain rice for it's goodness.

---

3 tbsp olive oil

1 red onion, sliced

1 red (bell) pepper, deseeded and thinly sliced

4 cloves garlic, crushed

2 skinless chicken breasts, cut into small strips

1 tsp smoked paprika

1 tsp ground cumin

1 tsp ground coriander

250g/7 oz wholegrain rice

400ml/14 fl oz passata or tinned chopped tomatoes

1–2 tsp chipotle paste, depending on whether you want it spicy or not

1 x 400g/14 oz tin kidney or black beans, drained

155g/5½ oz sweetcorn

1 bunch of coriander (cilantro)

flaked sea salt and freshly ground black pepper

lime wedges, to serve

Time taken 1¼ hours / **Serves** 4–6

Preheat the oven to 180°C/160°C fan/350°F/gas 4.

Heat the oil in a large casserole dish and add the onion and red pepper. Sauté for 5 minutes to soften, then add the garlic, chicken, smoked paprika, cumin and coriander. Fry for a further 2 minutes for the chicken to turn opaque.

Stir in the rice, passata or tomatoes, chipotle paste, kidney or black beans, sweetcorn and 600ml/1 pint/2½ cups water. Season well with salt and pepper. Roughly chop the coriander stalks and add to the pan. Reserve the leaves for serving.

Bring to a simmer, cover with a lid and place in the oven for about 45–50 minutes until the rice is tender and the liquid has been absorbed.

Serve scattered with coriander leaves and lime wedges to squeeze over the top.

Flexible

Vegetarian/vegan: *omit the chicken and double the amount of beans instead.*

Upgrade: *heat 1 tablespoon olive oil in a small frying pan. Add 1½ teaspoons each of chilli powder, ground cumin and smoked paprika. Cook for 30 seconds and remove from the heat. Add to a bowl with 2 teaspoons tomato ketchup, ½ teaspoon Worcestershire sauce and 1 teaspoon marmite. Mix in 200g/7 oz soft butter and serve at room temperature with the chicken and rice.*

Flavour swap: *add a chunky avocado salsa. Dice 1–2 ripe avocados, 1 ripe tomato, ½ red onion and ½ red or green chilli. Mix with some chopped coriander, juice of ½ lime, pinch of salt and a good splash of oil.*

Rice swap: *if you switch wholegrain rice for white rice you will need to cut the cooking time down by about 20 minutes, and cut the added water down by 200ml/7 fl oz/scant 1 cup as well.*

Salmon and vegetable biryani

with cucumber and mint yoghurt

This is a perfectly balanced meal, all cooked together in super-quick time, for the whole family to enjoy. It's not too spicy, if you choose a mild curry paste, and it's gluten- and dairy-free. Brown or white cooked rice can be used, and for a time-saving hack, use the pre-cooked packs.

300g/10½ oz combined weight of broccoli
    and cauliflower, cut into bite-size florets
2 tbsp sunflower or groundnut oil
1 large onion, finely sliced
400g/14 oz skinless salmon fillet, cut
    into 2cm/¾ inch chunks
4 cloves garlic, crushed
2 tsp grated ginger
3 tbsp curry paste
1 tsp ground turmeric
handful sultanas
500g/1 lb 2 oz cooked basmati rice, brown
    or white (pre-packaged is perfect)
juice ½ large lemon
25g/1 oz toasted flaked coconut
    or almonds
flaked sea salt

For the yoghurt
6 tbsp natural yoghurt
3 tbsp chopped mint
¼ cucumber, seeds removed and
    finely chopped

Time taken 30 minutes / **Serves** 4

Steam or lightly boil the broccoli and cauliflower until just tender.

Meanwhile, mix together the yoghurt, mint and cucumber. Season with a pinch of salt and set aside.

Heat the oil in a large frying pan and sauté the onion for 8 minutes until soft and becoming golden.

Add the chunks of salmon, garlic, ginger, curry paste, turmeric, sultanas and 4 tablespoons water. Toss around in the pan for about 2 minutes before adding the cooked rice and steamed vegetables. Gently stir around in the pan until the salmon is just cooked through and the rice is piping hot.

Stir in the lemon juice and season with a pinch of salt. Scatter with coconut or almonds and serve with the cucumber and mint yoghurt.

Flexible

Vegetarian: *diced paneer, halloumi or tofu all work very well when added to the pan. Fry until they take on some colour first, adding to the pan just before the 4 tablespoons water.*

Flavour swap: *smoked mackerel, hot-smoked salmon or trout are delicious alternatives to fresh salmon. Flake into the pan when you add the lemon juice and toss around to heat through.*

Meat-lovers: *if you've any leftover roast chicken, turkey or lamb from your weekend roast, use in place of the salmon.*

Sticky pomegranate chicken

with jewelled quinoa

Wow – the tangy, sweet, mouth-watering glaze you get when cooking the chicken is out of this world. You can cook the chicken straightaway but if you can do some advance planning it's definitely best to leave it overnight to marinate. Chicken thighs are best as they stay nice and juicy, and opt for larger ones if possible.

This colourful salad pairs well with the chicken, and if there happen to be any leftovers, add in some feta and enjoy as a lunch the next day.

For the chicken

8 decent-sized chicken thighs, boneless

3 tbsp pomegranate molasses

2 tbsp tomato purée

2 cloves garlic, crushed or grated

1 tsp ground coriander

1 tsp ground cumin

1 tsp caster (superfine) sugar

juice ½ lemon

2 tbsp olive oil

handful pistachio nuts, roughly chopped

For the salad

200g/7 oz quinoa

500ml/17 fl oz/2 cups vegetable stock

4 tbsp pomegranate seeds

4 spring onions (scallions), finely chopped

2 sticks celery, finely diced

½ cucumber, seeds removed and finely
    diced

1 red (bell) pepper, seeds removed and
    finely diced

3 tbsp extra virgin olive oil

juice of 1 lemon

large handful each of mint, parsley,
    coriander (cilantro), chopped

flaked sea salt and freshly ground
    black pepper

Time taken 1¼ hours + at least 30 minutes marinating / **Serves** 4

Mix the chicken with the pomegranate molasses, tomato purée, garlic, coriander, cumin, sugar, lemon juice and olive oil. Leave to marinate in the fridge for about 30 minutes or overnight if you have the time.

Put the quinoa in a saucepan and cover with the stock. Bring to the boil and cook at a fast boil for 2 minutes. Cover with a lid and cook over a low heat for 10 minutes, without removing the lid. Remove from the heat, keeping the lid on, and sit for 5 minutes. By now the quinoa will have absorbed all of the stock and will be light and fluffy when you run a fork through to separate the grains. Leave to cool.

To cook the chicken, preheat the oven to 220°C/200°C fan/425°F/ gas 7. Transfer the thighs, skin side up, and all of the marinade into a roasting tray just big enough to fit the thighs in one layer. Bake for 35–40 minutes until the chicken is sticky and golden, basting halfway through and adding a splash of water if the juices are cooking too quickly.

While the chicken cooks, toss the cooled quinoa with the all of the remaining salad ingredients, reserving some of the pomegranate seeds for serving. Season to taste.

Once the chicken is cooked, serve with the jewelled quinoa salad, and scatter over the reserved pomegranate seeds and chopped pistachios.

Flexible

Vegetarian: *Sticky Pomegranate Aubergine and Feta is a delicious meat-free alternative. Mix together the marinade ingredients. Cut 2 aubergines (eggplants) and 2 red onions into wedges. Put directly in a roasting tray along with 200g/7 oz feta cheese cut into large chunks. Gently mix with the marinade as above. Roast for about 30 minutes, basting occasionally, until tender and golden.*

Thai green squash and tofu curry traybake

For meat-free days this is a fantastic one-pan wonder. So simple to prepare with minimal washing-up, making it a perfect mid-week meal. If you think tofu isn't your thing, do give this a try. When it's roasted it takes on a firmer texture and absorbs the aromatic flavour from the Thai curry paste.

I find this filling enough as it is, but Steamed Basmati Rice (see page 124) and Cucumber, Mango and Peanut Salad (see page 136) would be good accompaniments.

---

1 butternut squash, about 1kg/
   2 lb 4 oz, cut into 2–3cm/1–1½ inch
   chunks (peeled if preferred)
3 banana shallots, cut into chunks
3 tbsp sunflower oil
2 tbsp Thai green curry paste
   (more or less depending on the
   brand and your tastes)
1 x 400ml/14 fl oz tin coconut milk
250g/9 oz extra-firm tofu, diced
100g/3½ oz baby corn, halved on an angle
100g/3½ oz sugar snap peas, halved
1 bunch coriander (cilantro), chopped
juice 1 lime
light soy sauce or flaked sea salt
   (or fish sauce for non-vegetarian)
lime wedges, to serve

Time taken 1 hour 10 minutes / **Serves** 4

Preheat the oven to 200°C/180C fan/400°F/gas 6.

Put the squash, shallots, oil and curry paste in a large baking tray, and toss everything together well.

Bake for 35–40 minutes, turning the vegetables occasionally, until the squash is cooked through and becoming golden.

Stir in the coconut milk, tofu, baby corn, sugar snap peas, half the coriander and lime juice. Season with soy sauce or salt and return to the oven for a further 15 minutes.

Once cooked, scatter over the remaining coriander and check for seasoning. Serve with lime wedges to squeeze over.

Flexible

Pescatarian: replace the tofu with 350–400g / 12–14 oz raw peeled prawns added to the pan for the final 15 minutes of cooking time. Season with fish sauce.

Meat-lovers: put 6–8 chicken thigh fillets in with the squash and omit the tofu.

Tandoori rice salad

This is great for summer entertaining. You can choose whatever you like to put in the tandoori marinade, making it suitable for pescatarians, vegetarians, meat eaters or vegans (providing you use a plant-based yoghurt). Prepare well ahead of time and leave in the fridge in order for the spices to work their magic.

For the colourful aromatic salad, I like to use brown basmati rice for the nuttiness it gives, not to mention the added goodness.

Tandoori

3 tbsp tandoori curry paste
5 tbsp natural yoghurt
400–500g/14 oz–1 lb 2 oz meat, fish, veg, paneer or tofu (see Flexible), cut into bite-size pieces
25g/1 oz butter, melted

Salad

250g/9 oz brown basmati rice
75g/2¾ oz sultanas
juice of 1 lemon
1 red onion, finely sliced
75g/2¾ oz flaked almonds
1½ tsp cumin seeds
2 medium-large carrots, peeled and coarsely grated or very finely shredded
1 small bunch of coriander (cilantro), roughly chopped
2 tsp soft light brown sugar
4 tbsp olive oil or rapeseed (canola) oil
flaked sea salt

To serve

poppadoms
raita and/or mango chutney

Time taken 45 minutes + marinating for a few hours or overnight / **Serves** 4

Mix together the tandoori paste and yoghurt in a large bowl. Add the meat, fish or vegetarian option to the marinade, cover and put in the fridge to marinate for a few hours, up to overnight.

To make the salad, cook the rice in a large pan of boiling salted water according to the packet instructions, adding the sultanas for the last 5 minutes of cooking time. Drain and leave to steam dry and cool in a large sieve or bowl, with a clean tea towel over the top.

While the rice is cooking, pour the lemon juice over the onion. Season with a pinch of salt and set aside.

Heat a small frying pan and gently toast the flaked almonds and cumin seeds together until the almonds are golden.

Once the rice is cool, transfer to a large bowl and stir in the carrot, coriander, toasted almonds and cumin seeds.

Add the sugar and olive oil to the lemony onion and stir until the sugar has dissolved. Pour over the rice salad and mix well.

Preheat the grill to high. Transfer your tandoori-marinated ingredients to a foil-lined baking tray. Grill on a top shelf for the suggested timings below until golden and cooked through. Baste with a little butter at the end. Serve hot with the rice salad and poppadoms, raita and chutney, if liked.

Flexible

Boneless chicken thigh or breast, cut into chunks: *grill for 10 minutes, turning occasionally. Insert a skewer and if its cooked, juices should run clear.*

Lamb chops, steaks or rump: *grill for 10 minutes, turning halfway.*

Fish fillets: *ideally firm thick fillets such as cod, haddock, salmon, pollock etc. Grill for 5–6 minutes, turning once.*

Prawns, peeled: *grill for 4–5 minutes, turning occasionally.*

Paneer, halloumi or tofu: *cut into cubes and grill on the middle shelf for 4–5 minutes, turning once.*

Cauliflower florets: *grill for 10 minutes, turning occasionally.*

Crunchy chicken and Parmesan schnitzel

Time taken 30 minutes / **Serves** 4

This is a good recipe for your children to help with. They'll love doing the messy bits of coating the chicken in the crumbs. Set up a production line of flour, egg and crumbs to dip into and the job's a doddle. Once coated, the schnitzels can sit in the fridge for a few hours or can be frozen and defrosted before cooking.

I urge you to use the dried panko breadcrumbs if you can as they will give you a crisp end result with juicier chicken inside.

———————————————————

4 chicken breasts, skinless
50g/1¾ oz plain (all-purpose) flour
2 eggs, beaten
75g/2¾ oz panko breadcrumbs or very
   dry white bread, blitzed into crumbs
½ tsp paprika
3 tbsp finely grated Parmesan
grated zest of ½ lemon
sunflower or rapeseed (canola) oil,
   for frying
lemon wedges, to serve
flaked sea salt

Place a chicken breast between 2 sheets of baking parchment or cling film. Using a rolling pin, gently bash until it's evenly flattened to around 0.5–1cm/ ¼–½ inch thick. Repeat with the remaining chicken breasts.

Put the flour, eggs and breadcrumbs in 3 wide shallow bowls or plates. Season the flour with a good pinch of salt and stir in the paprika. Mix the lemon zest and Parmesan into the breadcrumbs.

Dip a chicken breast into the flour, then the egg, making sure it's fully coated, and finally into the Parmesan crumbs, also making sure it's evenly coated. Repeat with the remaining chicken breasts.

If you've time, chill in the fridge for 30 minutes, for the coating to 'set' around the chicken. It's not essential but just makes the cooking process a little easier and guarantees a crunchier finish.

Heat enough oil to generously cover the base of 1 or 2 large frying pans. If you've only 1, you'll need to cook the chicken in batches, so it's worth setting the oven to low and keeping the schnitzels warm while you cook the remaining ones.

Fry the chicken for 3–4 minutes each side, over a medium heat, until golden and crispy. Drain on kitchen paper before serving with wedges of lemon to squeeze over.

Flexible

Gluten-free: gluten-free flour and breadcrumbs work well for this recipe. Crushed gluten-free cornflakes, tortilla chips or polenta can also be used for adding a crisp crust.

Vegetarian: coat sticks of halloumi in the flour, egg and breadcrumbs (minus the Parmesan). Rather than shallow fry as above, they are best deep fried in oil. Be warned, they are exceptionally moorish!

Flavour swap: swap the paprika for any dried herb or spice, such as Cajun blend, curry powder, chilli powder, oregano, smoked paprika or mustard powder. Switch the Parmesan and lemon for desiccated coconut and lime zest, and use chilli powder instead of paprika.

Red apple slaw

A tasty coleslaw recipe is always good to have on hand for any time of year.

––––––––––––––––––––––––––

2 red skinned apples, halved, cored and
    cut into matchsticks
¼ red or white cabbage, very finely sliced
1 carrot, peeled and coarsely grated
1 small red onion, very thinly sliced
2 sticks celery, finely sliced
1 small fennel, finely sliced
juice 1 lemon
2 tbsp tahini
2 tbsp mayonnaise
1 tsp honey
1 tsp ground cumin
3 tbsp natural yoghurt
flaked sea salt and freshly ground
    black pepper
50g/2¾ oz pomegranate seeds
2 tsp toasted sesame seeds

Time taken 20 minutes / **Serves** 6–8

Put the apple, cabbage, carrot, onion, celery and fennel in a mixing bowl and toss together.

In a separate bowl, mix together the lemon juice, tahini, mayonnaise, honey, cumin and yoghurt until smooth. Pour over the vegetables and mix well. Season with salt and pepper. Transfer to a serving bowl and scatter with pomegranate seeds and sesame seeds.

Flexible

Flavour swap: blend together 100g/3½ oz silken tofu, 3 tablespoons rice vinegar, 3 tablespoons white miso paste, 2 tablespoons pickled ginger, 1 small grated clove garlic, 1 tablespoon toasted sesame oil, 1 teaspoon flaked sea salt and 4 tablespoons cold water. Toss into prepared vegetables, such as white cabbage, carrot, spring onions (scallions), mooli and chopped coriander (cilantro). Scatter with sesame seeds.

Crunchy smashed potatoes

These olive oil roasties are a real crowd pleaser. It's the little crispy, salty, crunchy pieces of potato that are irresistible, making everyone want to go back for more, so do make sure you make plenty!

––––––––––––––––––––––––––

1 kg/2 lb 4 oz new potatoes
olive oil
4 cloves garlic, peeled and flattened
    with the back of a knife
a sprig of fresh rosemary
flaked sea salt

Time taken 45 minutes / **Serves** 4

Preheat the oven to 200°C/180°C fan/400°F/gas 6.

Cook the potatoes in boiling salted water for 10–12 minutes until they are almost cooked through. Drain and cool for a few minutes. Transfer them to a roasting tray and crush each one lightly so they are just holding their shape but are crumbling at the edges.

Pour over a generous amount of olive oil and toss to coat. Add the garlic and rosemary and bake for about 40 minutes, tossing occasionally until golden and crunchy. Season with salt and serve.

Flexible

Flavour swap: add 1 teaspoon ground cumin, 1 teaspoon ground coriander, ½ teaspoon chilli powder and ½ teaspoon ground turmeric to the roasting tray with the oil, potatoes and garlic. Season when cooked.

Gnocchi, aubergine and tomato bake

We all need a few quick and easy weeknight suppers to rely on and this could soon become one of your regulars. It's well worth keeping a bag of fresh gnocchi in the fridge for emergency suppers. Double up on quantities and make a couple of trays if you've an army of kids to feed. If you want to make it go even further serve with some garlic bread and a big green salad.

---

1 onion, sliced

1 medium-large aubergine (eggplant), cut into bite-size chunks

3 tbsp olive oil, plus extra for drizzling

1 x 400g/14 oz tin chopped tomatoes

1 tbsp tomato purée

2 cloves garlic, grated or crushed

1 tsp caster (superfine) sugar

1 tsp balsamic vinegar

handful chopped basil

450g/1 lb fresh gnocchi

200g/7 oz mozzarella

flaked sea salt and freshly ground black pepper

Time taken 1 hour / **Serves** 4

Preheat the oven to 220°C/200°C fan/425°F/gas 7.

Put the onion and aubergine in a roasting tray or baking dish big enough for them to sit in a single layer. Toss in the oil and season with salt and pepper. Roast in the oven for 20 minutes, turning halfway for even cooking, until they are lightly golden.

Mix together the chopped tomatoes, tomato purée, garlic, sugar, balsamic, basil and 100ml/3½ fl oz/scant ½ cup water.

Remove the tray from the oven and pour in the tomato mixture, add the gnocchi and stir around to coat in the sauce.

Tear the mozzarella into pieces and dot around the tray. Drizzle with olive oil and add a twist of pepper. Return the tray to the oven for 30 minutes until the sauce is bubbling and the top is golden.

Flexible

Upgrade: *you can add a variety of ingredients to this to make it different every time you serve it. Add diced chorizo or spicy Italian sausage with the onions and aubergine (eggplant). Or add some chilli, olives, capers or anchovies to the sauce. I also like to scatter in some tinned flaked tuna or prawns when adding the gnocchi.*

Veggie-lover: *for added veggies, stir some spinach through the sauce or throw in a handful of green beans.*

Cheese-lover: *try a different cheese such as taleggio, ricotta, dolcelatte or a generous scattering of Parmesan. The options really are endless.*

One-pot goat's cheese, spinach and walnut pasta

There's nothing more satisfying than a big bowl of pasta and it tends to be a go-to in many households when something easy and effortless is required. And effortless is the key word in this recipe, as all the ingredients go into one pot and cook in 15 minutes. What's not to love about that?

Do note that this recipe serves two people. You can increase quantities to serve four, however, you will need a pretty big saucepan to allow the pasta to cook properly and not become stodgy.

———————————————

2 tbsp extra virgin olive oil, plus extra for drizzling

1 small onion, sliced

200g/7 oz pasta shapes (such as penne or fusilli)

2 cloves garlic, crushed

150g/5½ oz soft mild goat's cheese, broken into pieces

50g/1¾ oz walnut halves, roughly chopped

700ml/1¼ fl oz/scant 3 cups hot vegetable stock

grated fresh nutmeg, for sprinkling

100g/3½ oz baby spinach leaves

flaked sea salt and freshly ground black pepper

grated zest of ½ lemon, to serve

Time taken 25 minutes / **Serves** 2

Heat the oil in a medium-large saucepan. Add the onion and sauté gently for about 5–6 minutes until softened and light golden.

Add the pasta, garlic, goat's cheese, walnuts and vegetable stock. Stir briefly and season with a generous grating of nutmeg and some salt and pepper.

Increase the heat to high and bring to the boil. Reduce to a simmer and cook, without a lid, over a medium heat, for 12–15 minutes, stirring occasionally, until the pasta is just cooked with a little bite (al dente). By now the stock will have absorbed into the pasta and created a lightly creamy sauce.

Stir the spinach through the pasta to wilt and taste for seasoning, adding more if needed. Serve in 2 bowls garnished with lemon zest, a grating of nutmeg, twist of pepper and a drizzle of extra virgin olive oil.

Flexible

Flavour swap: *an even simpler version with fewer ingredients and ideal for fussy palates. Place 200g / 7 oz dried spaghetti or linguine in a large saucepan with 1 sliced onion, 2 crushed or grated cloves garlic, 1 chopped anchovy, 2–3 chopped ripe tomatoes, 2 tablespoons tomato purée, some roughly chopped basil, 2 tablespoons extra virgin olive oil and 600ml / 1 pint / 2½ cups veg stock. Bring to the boil, pushing the spaghetti under the water, then simmer for 15 minutes, stirring occasionally. Stir in 2 tablespoons mascarpone or cream cheese, season to taste and serve with Parmesan.*

Baked Tuscan bean and sausage stew

This ultimate comfort food recipe is one you can turn to when all you want is something quick and easy that you can throw into one pot. For the best results use some good-quality pork sausages, ideally with some Italian flavourings such as fennel seeds. If you can't find any you could always add a scattering of fennel seeds or a sliced fennel bulb with the onions.

---

2 tbsp olive oil

8 chunky pork sausages, each one
   cut into 2–3 pieces

2 onions, sliced

1 red (bell) pepper, deseeded and sliced

2 sticks celery, thickly sliced

¼ tsp dried chilli flakes

4 sprigs fresh rosemary

2 x 400g/14 oz tins beans such as borlotti,
   cannellini, pinto or haricot, drained

2 x 400g/14 oz tins chopped tomatoes

2 tbsp dark brown sugar

1 tbsp red wine vinegar or cider vinegar

flaked sea salt and freshly ground
   black pepper

To serve (optional)

crusty bread or mash

buttered greens

Time taken 1¼ hours / **Serves** 4

Preheat the oven to 200°C/180°C fan/400°F/gas 6.

Heat the oil in a fairly shallow ovenproof pan or heavy roasting tray and quickly brown the sausages all over to just give them colour on the outside but not cook them all the way through.

Add the onions and cook for a couple of minutes to also give them some colour, then add all the remaining ingredients. Season with salt and pepper and stir around to mix. Cover with a lid or if you don't have one, then a baking tray on top will be just fine.

Bake for 30 minutes, then remove the lid, stir everything around and return to the oven without a lid for a further 15–20 minutes until the sauce has thickened.

Serve with crusty bread or mash, and some greens such as buttered steamed cabbage or green beans.

Flexible

Gluten-free: *the sausages are the only ingredient in this recipe that is likely to contain gluten, so make sure you use gluten-free ones.*

Vegetarian/vegan: *vegetarian or vegan sausages won't hold themselves well cooking for so long in the sauce, so you are better to cook them separately until golden, then add them to the stew for the final 15–20 minutes of cooking.*

Tikka traybake

Traybakes are a lifesaver when you need a low-maintenance meal. This recipe is medium on the spice front, as it uses tikka masala paste. You can increase or decrease the heat of the spice paste according to preference. If you're cooking for a mixture of tastes, I suggest you make it mild in the first place, and for anyone wanting more heat, they can scatter some fresh or dried chilli on their own serving. That way it's happy families all round!

---

2 large onions, cut into 3cm/1¼ inch pieces

1 large aubergine (eggplant), cut into 3cm/1¼ inch pieces

2 sweet potatoes, peeled and cut into 3cm/1¼ inch pieces

½ cauliflower, broken into florets

450g/1 lb skinless chicken thigh fillets, cut into chunks

sunflower or rapeseed (canola) oil, for cooking

6 ripe tomatoes, roughly chopped

4 tbsp tikka masala curry paste (or curry paste of your choice)

1 x 400ml/14 fl oz tin coconut milk

small bunch of chopped coriander (cilantro)

1 tsp nigella (onion) seeds

flaked sea salt and freshly ground black pepper

Time taken 1½ hours / **Serves** 4

Preheat the oven to 220°C/200°C fan/425°F/gas 6.

Place the onions, aubergine, sweet potatoes and cauliflower in a single layer in a large roasting tray (or 2 smaller ones if necessary).

Add the chicken and enough oil to lightly coat everything. Season with salt and pepper and roast for 40 minutes, turning a couple of times throughout.

Add the tomatoes and curry paste. Toss around, and return to the oven for a further 20–30 minutes, again turning everything a couple of times for even cooking, until the veggies are tender and nicely golden.

Transfer the roasting tray to the hob and put over a medium-high heat. Pour in three-quarters of the coconut milk and stir until it comes to a simmer. Add the remaining coconut milk for a saucier finish if preferred. Cook for 5 minutes. Season to taste.

If serving straight away, stir through most of the coriander. Alternatively, loosely cover with foil and return to the oven set to about 150°C/130°C fan/300°F/gas 2 to keep hot.

Serve scattered with nigella seeds and the remaining coriander.

Flexible

Vegetarian/vegan: *swap the chicken for 450g/1 lb diced paneer cheese or 2 x 400g/4 oz tins drained chickpeas. Rather than adding at the start of the recipe, add to the roasting tray at the same time you add the curry paste and tomatoes.*

Pescatarian: *swap the chicken for 400g/14 oz raw king prawns. Season with salt and add to the pan when you add the coconut milk. Simmer for 5 minutes, until they are cooked through and pink in colour.*

Cajun salmon and sweet potato fish cakes

This is one of those fantastic prepare-ahead recipes. Once shaped and coated in crumbs, the fishcakes can sit in the fridge for a couple of days if need be.

I've made many fishcakes with white potatoes using leftover mash, which works wonders, but here I am using sweet potatoes that are roasted to bring out their natural sweetness. While the oven is on, the salmon is coated in punchy Cajun spices and lime juice in a foil parcel.

---

3 sweet potatoes
400–450g/14 oz–1 lb salmon fillet
1 tbsp olive oil
1½ tbsp Cajun spice
1 tsp flaked sea salt
grated zest and juice of 1 lime
4 spring onions (scallions), finely chopped
small handful chopped coriander
   (cilantro)
100g/3½ oz plain (all-purpose) flour
2 eggs, lightly beaten
100g/3½ oz dried white breadcrumbs,
   ideally panko
sunflower oil, for shallow frying
flaked sea salt and freshly ground
   black pepper
lime wedges, to serve

Time taken 1½ hours + at least 30 minutes chilling / **Serves** 4

Preheat the oven to 200°C/180°C fan/400°F/gas 6.

Wash the sweet potatoes and prick each one several times with a fork. Bake for 45–60 minutes until they are tender.

Meanwhile, sit the salmon on a large piece of foil. Rub in the olive oil, Cajun spice, salt and squeeze over the lime juice, reserving the zest for later. Seal the foil to make a loose parcel and sit on a baking tray. Bake for 15 minutes while the sweet potatoes are in the oven.

Scoop the flesh of the roast sweet potatoes into a bowl and roughly mash. Flake the cooked salmon on top and pour over any cooking juices from the foil. Add the lime zest, spring onions and coriander. Season with salt and gently mix together.

Chill in the fridge until cool, then shape into fishcakes – anything between 4–8, depending on what size you fancy.

Dust each fishcake in flour, then dip in the beaten egg and finish by coating each one in breadcrumbs, shaking off any excess. If you have time, chill in the fridge for 20–30 minutes to make them easier to fry.

Add enough sunflower oil to generously cover the base of a large frying pan and place over a medium heat. Add the fish cakes and fry for about 3 minutes on each side until golden and crisp. Drain on kitchen paper and serve hot with lime wedges to squeeze over, a green salad, green veg or Rainbow Fries (see page 131).

Flexible

Gluten-free: *use gluten-free flour and breadcrumbs, or alternatively you can substitute the breadcrumbs with crushed gluten-free cornflakes.*

Cajun spice: *you can quite easily make your own Cajun spice mix if you've already got the spices. Simply mix together 1 tablespoon each of paprika and garlic salt with 1 teaspoon each of ground cumin, ground black or white pepper, cayenne pepper, oregano and thyme.*

Miso cod and fried rice

The rich umami flavour of miso in the sticky Japanese style marinade is perfect for any fish. Here I've used cod, though I'll often use salmon or even sea bass. Just bear in mind the thinner the fish, the more the cooking time will need to be reduced.

You'll notice I add mayonnaise to the rice; it may seem a little odd, but it's a great way to prevent rice grains from sticking to both the pan and to each other. You don't taste the mayonnaise – it just makes the end result richer in flavour.

For the cod

4 cod fillets, skin on or off

3 tbsp white miso paste

3 tbsp soy sauce

3 tbsp honey

1 tbsp rice wine vinegar

1 tsp toasted sesame seeds

1 red chilli, finely sliced (optional)

For the rice

1 tbsp sunflower oil

2–3 large handfuls finely shredded green cabbage

400–500g/14 oz–1 lb 2 oz cooked rice

2 tbsp mayonnaise

1 bunch spring onions (scallions), finely chopped

1 tsp grated ginger

2 eggs, beaten

soy sauce

Time taken 30 minutes + at least 30 minutes marinating / **Serves** 4

To prepare the cod, pat the fillets dry with kitchen paper and put in a shallow bowl with the miso, soy sauce, honey and rice wine vinegar. Mix well to coat the fish all over and leave in the fridge to marinate for 30 minutes, or longer of you have the time (up to 8 hours will be just fine).

When ready to cook, heat your grill on a medium-high setting. Transfer the cod and any marinade to a foil-lined baking tray or suitable ovenproof serving dish. Put under the grill for 10 minutes until the fish is just cooked through and nicely golden on top.

Meanwhile, for the fried rice, mix the mayonnaise into the rice to lightly coat the grains.

Heat the oil in a wok or frying pan. Stir-fry the cabbage for about 2–3 minutes until it's starting to soften. Add the spring onions and ginger, stir-frying for a further minute.

Add the rice and toss around for a few minutes until the rice is completely heated through. Make a well in the middle and pour in the eggs. Allow them to partially scramble, then stir and toss into the rice. Season with soy sauce.

Serve the cod sprinkled with sesame seeds and scattered with and chilli, if using, alongside the fried rice.

Flexible

Vegetarian/vegan: miso aubergine (eggplant) is melt-in-the-mouth delicious, and both vegetarian and vegan friendly. Slice an aubergine in half lengthways, and diagonally score a lattice pattern into the flesh, taking care not to cut all the way through. Brush with a little oil and bake at 200°C / 180°C fan / 400°F / gas 6 for 20–25 minutes, turning halfway through until tender. Sit cut side up. Spoon over the marinade mixture and grill for just a few minutes until golden, basting with the marinade once or twice.

Cheese, onion and potato pie

Sometimes you just need comfort food in its purest form. This isn't really a pie, but more of a bake and reminds me of a fantastic one I used to love as a child. I like to make it with Cheddar, but you can use almost any cheese you like – grated or crumbled. Stilton or gruyère are also favourites of mine, but only when I'm in the mood for a stronger flavour.

1kg/2 lb 4 oz potatoes, peeled and
    quartered
60g/2 oz butter
2 onions, thinly sliced
150ml/5 fl oz/²/₃ cup milk
300g/10½ oz mature Cheddar, double
    Gloucester or red Leicester cheese,
    grated
1–2 tsp wholegrain or English mustard
flaked sea salt and freshly ground
    black pepper
2–3 tomatoes, sliced

Time taken 50 minutes / **Serves** 4

Preheat the oven to 200°C/180°C fan/400°F/gas 6.

Cook the potatoes in boiling salted water for 15–20 minutes until tender.

While the potatoes are cooking, melt the butter in a pan and gently sauté the onion for 8–10 minutes until lightly golden and turning sticky. Add the milk to the pan and heat until it's almost boiling.

Drain the potatoes and return back to the pan they were cooked in. Let the excess steam evaporate, then mash really well until smooth. Briskly stir in the milk and onions, three-quarters of the cheese, the mustard and season to taste.

Transfer to a buttered ovenproof dish, scatter over the remaining cheese and lay the tomato slices on top.

Sit on a baking tray and bake for 20–25 minutes until the top is bubbling and lightly golden.

Flexible

Vegan: *you don't have to rule this recipe out if you are vegan. You can quite easily swap the butter, milk and cheese for plant-based vegan alternatives.*

Flavour swap: *if you fancy experimenting, try adding some different ingredients. Diced ham, cooked crispy bacon, sliced salami or chorizo; flakes of smoked mackerel or hot smoked salmon; sautéed mushrooms or red (bell) peppers; or chopped herbs, such as thyme, basil or chives.*

sides and accompaniments

Perfect steamed basmati rice

Follow this method for cooking basmati and you should have perfect, fluffy rice every time. The rice is cooked in a measured amount of water so that by the time it's ready, all the liquid has been absorbed, and the rice steamed, meaning there is no draining of gloopy, starchy water required. As a general rule you require 1-part rice to 2-parts water, and for one average portion weigh 75g/2¾ oz per person, with 150ml/5 fl oz water.

300g/10½ oz basmati rice,
   washed
600ml/1 pint/½ cup cold water
flaked sea salt

Time taken 18 minutes / **Serves** 4 (scale up or down as needed)

Put the rice in a medium-large saucepan. Add the water and a good pinch of salt. Place the pan over a high heat until the water is bubbling, then let it boil furiously for 1 minute. Cover with a tight-fitting lid, turn the heat to low and leave to cook for 10 minutes, without lifting the lid at all.

After 10 minutes, turn off the heat, but you must keep the lid firmly in place because the rice will carry on cooking. Leave for 5 minutes before removing the lid (though it can stay hot for up to 20 minutes if you leave the lid on). Remove the lid and run a fork through the rice to reveal wonderfully light and fluffy cooked rice.

Flexible

Upgrade: You can add flavours to the rice – dried spices such as 8–10 cloves, 4–6 cardamom pods, 1 cinnamon stick, 2–3 bay leaves, strips of lemon zest, or even use stock instead of water.

Saffron baked rice

An alternative to steaming rice on the hob is to bake it and I'm sure this could quite easily become one of your go-to side dishes that works well with pretty much anything else on the table.

3 tbsp butter or olive oil
1 onion, finely chopped
2 cloves garlic, grated or crushed
good pinch of saffron strands
4 cardamom pods
1 stick cinnamon
50g/1¾ oz sultanas
½ tsp flaked sea salt
300g/10½ oz basmati rice,
   washed
600ml/1 pint/2½ cups hot
   vegetable stock

To serve
handful of fresh herbs such as dill,
   parsley and/or coriander (cilantro)

Time taken 55 minutes / **Serves** 4

Preheat the oven to 180°C/160°C fan/350°F/gas 4. Melt the butter in an ovenproof baking dish, about 1.5 litre/2¾ pint capacity, placed over a low heat. Add the onion and gently cook for up to 10 minutes until it is golden and sticky. Add the garlic, saffron, cardamom, cinnamon, sultanas and salt for the last couple of minutes.

Increase the heat and stir in the rice, mixing it around until it is fully coated in the buttery onion. Pour in the stock, bring to a simmer and cover with tight-fitting foil or a lid. Bake for 25 minutes. Once cooked, remove from the oven and set aside for 10 minutes without removing the foil or lid. Remove the foil and run a fork through to separate the grains. Scatter with fresh herbs and serve.

Flexible

Cajun Baked Rice: sauté 1 finely chopped celery stick with the onion. Add 1½ tablespoons Cajun spice, zest of ½ lime and 2 crushed cloves garlic. Add the rice, stock and 175g/6 oz sweetcorn. Stir through chopped coriander to serve.

Chinese Spiced: swap half of the butter for sesame oil. Add 1 cinnamon stick, 1 star anise, 2 teaspoons ground coriander and 2 cloves crushed garlic. Add the rice and stock. Season with soy sauce and stir through chopped coriander to serve.

Creamy salad dressing or dip

I am a fan of using silken tofu blended into sauces and dressings, as it not only adds a smooth rich creaminess but loads of nutrient-rich goodness too. I'll use it at least once a week blended into the Flexible Tomato Sauce (see page 139) but here I am using it in a very versatile dressing for salads or roasted veg, or a dip for vegetable crudité. Get ahead by making this up to 4 days in advance and storing it in the fridge.

200g/7 oz silken tofu

4 tbsp tahini

4 tbsp extra virgin olive oil

finely grated zest and juice of 1 lemon

1 tsp ground cumin

1 small clove garlic

1 tsp flaked sea salt

2 tbsp toasted sesame seeds

Time taken 30 minutes / **Serves** 4

Blend together all the ingredients, apart from the sesame seeds, until smooth.

Add enough cold water to give you your preferred consistency, keeping it thick to use for dipping into, or loosen to a pouring consistency for dressing salad leaves.

Check for seasoning and adjust if needed.

Serve sprinkled with the sesame seeds.

Flexible

Flavour swap: here's a simple yet very tasty salad dressing recipe. Put 100ml / 3½ fl oz extra virgin olive oil, 100ml / 3½ fl oz sunflower oil, 2 tablespoons white wine vinegar, 1 tablespoon lemon juice, 2 teaspoons runny honey, 1 teaspoon Dijon Mustard, 1 small clove of garlic, peeled and cut in half, flaked sea salt and freshly ground black pepper in a screw-top jar and shake really well to combine. Use straightaway or keep at room temperature for a few weeks (removing the garlic after 1 week otherwise it becomes too strong).

Flavoured butters 3 ways

with corn on the cob

Here are three of my family's favourite flavoured butters that I'll quite often have in the fridge ready for when we want to have a quick starter, tasty side dish or even a cheeky snack throughout the day. These butters are equally as delicious melted over corn on the cob, served with baked potatoes, spread into a sliced baguette and baked (think garlic bread), or to quickly fry fillets of fish or prawns. Use your imagination and use on, in and with whatever you and your family fancy. Any unused butter keeps for a good few weeks in the fridge, as the butter acts as a preservative to the additional flavourings.

Time taken 15 minutes

To make the butters, mix together all the ingredients (aside from the Parmesan, bacon or sesame seeds) and keep at room temperature.

Bring a large saucepan of salted water to the boil. Add the corn on the cob (I generally do a whole corn per person), return to the boil and cook for 4–5 minutes and then drain.

Heat a frying pan and add as much butter as you fancy to coat the corn. When it has melted, add the corn, and using tongs, turn to coat in the flavoured melted butter.

Transfer to the serving dishes, pour over the butter from the pan and scatter with either Parmesan for the Kiev butter, fried bacon for the Tex Mex butter or sesame seeds for the tahini butter.

Kiev butter

125g/4½ oz butter
1 clove garlic, grated
2 tsp chopped chives
2 tsp chopped parsley
grated zest of ½ lemon
pinch of flaked sea salt
grated Parmesan, to serve

Tex Mex Butter

125g/4½ oz butter
1–2 tsp chipotle paste (depending
 on how much spice you want)
grated zest of ½ lime
1 tbsp chopped coriander (cilantro)
crispy fried bacon, to serve

Tahini Butter

125g/4½ oz butter
2 tbsp tahini
2 tbsp lime juice
1 tbsp soy sauce
toasted sesame seeds, to serve

Flexible

Vegan: As a plant based alternative to dairy butter blitz 250g/7oz nuts such as cashew, peanut or macadamia in a food processor for a few minutes, scraping the sides a couple of times, until you have a smooth, super creamy paste. Be patient as it will take a good few minutes. Add a little oil such as sunflower or coconut oil to make a softer consistency if you prefer. Continue to add your chosen flavours as per the recipes above.

Rainbow fries

Potato fries or chips are very hard to resist and loved worldwide. Yet you don't have to stick with just potatoes as you can make fries out of almost any root vegetable. The general rule of thumb for perfectly cooked rainbow fries is consistency of size. They don't all need to be a perfect shape, but they will benefit from being of a similar thickness, otherwise any smaller ones will end up burning and larger ones won't be cooked all the way through.

---

1 kg/2 lb 4 oz mixed root vegetables, such as orange, purple or yellow carrots, white or purple potatoes, sweet potatoes, celeriac, swede, parsnip.
3–4 tbsp sunflower, rapeseed (canola) or olive oil
flaked sea salt

Time taken 1 hour / **Serves** 4

Preheat the oven to 220°C/200°C fan/425°F/gas 7.

Wash the vegetables well and peel if you prefer, though it's not essential for oven-baked fries. Cut them all into even-size batons and put in a large bowl. Drizzle with the oil, season with salt and toss together so all of the batons are coated.

Spread out into a single layer on a large baking tray. Bake for about 35–45 minutes until golden and crisp on the outside but the centre is tender. Halfway through cooking, carefully turn the veggies for even cooking.

Leave to sit for a couple of minutes, as this will make them easier to lift from the tray, then using a fish slice transfer to a serving dish. Scatter with some more salt and eat hot.

Flexible

Flavour swap*: you can add a variety of flavourings during or after cooking to mix things up:*

Add 1–2 teaspoons smoked paprika (hot or sweet), garlic salt, spice blends such as Cajun, garam masala or Chinese five-spice, fresh or dried rosemary, oregano or thyme.

You can also use a fragrant oil such as chilli, truffle, rosemary or garlic.

Upgrade: *when cooked, the fries are delicious scattered with grated Parmesan or sumac.*

Soy-glazed greens

One of the best ways to cook green veg is quickly, so that they retain their colour, goodness and flavour. Here I'm stir-frying them in a wok, which has a nice wide surface area enabling the veggies to cook both speedily and evenly. Pretty much any green vegetable can be used. Let the seasons determine what you use. They are a perfect accompaniment to Asian-style dishes, such as Slow-Cooked Asian Beef (see page 76) or Miso Cod and Fried Rice (see page 119).

---

4 tbsp soy sauce

25g/1 oz soft brown sugar

2 tbsp lime juice

25g/1 oz coconut oil or butter

250g/7 oz green vegetables, such as green beans, broccoli, Brussels sprouts, cut into similar-sized pieces

1 tbsp toasted sesame seeds, to garnish

Time taken 15 minutes / **Serves** 4

Mix the soy sauce, sugar and lime juice together in a bowl along with 3 tablespoons water.

Heat a wok or large frying pan and melt the coconut oil or butter. Add the greens and toss around for a few minutes to start cooking. Pour in the soy glaze and cook for a few minutes until the vegetables are caramelised and tender, adding a splash or two of water if needed.

Scatter over sesame seeds to serve.

Flexible

Soy-Glazed Pork, Rice and Greens: *if you want to make this into a main course, fry 250g/9 oz pork mince (chicken, turkey or beef will also work) over a high heat in a drop of sesame oil, 2 cloves crushed or grated garlic and 2 teaspoons grated ginger. Fry until golden and crisp. Remove from the pan. Return the pan to the heat and cook the greens as per the recipe above. Add 250g/9 oz cooked rice (leftovers or pre-packed is great for this) towards the end to heat through, then finish by adding the pork. Serve with sesame seeds.*

Soy-Glazed Tofu, Rice and Greens: *to make it veggie, swap the pork for diced extra-firm tofu and fry with the greens. Add 250g/9 oz cooked rice (leftovers or pre-packed is great for this) towards the end to heat through. Serve with sesame seeds.*

Ratatouille traybake

*I'm a huge fan of a traybake, as it's
a wonderfully low-maintenance
form of cooking. Throw everything
in a roasting tray and let the oven
do all of the hard work for you. Here
I have taken all of the flavours of a
ratatouille, a classic French vegetable
stew, and roasted them instead.*

*Make up a big batch and use it up
during the week served hot or cold. How
about served as an accompaniment
to roasted fish or meat, tossed into
pasta, spooned on top of creamy
cheesy polenta, as a bruschetta or
pizza topping, mixed into couscous or
quinoa... The options are endless.*

---

1 large courgette (zucchini)

1 aubergine (eggplant)

1 red (bell) pepper

1 yellow (bell) pepper

1 red onion

400g/14 oz cherry tomatoes

4 garlic cloves, unpeeled

5 tbsp extra virgin olive oil

1 bunch basil, chopped

2 tbsp balsamic vinegar

flaked sea salt and freshly ground
   black pepper

Time taken 1 hour / **Serves** 4–6

Preheat the oven to 200°C/180°C fan/400°F/gas 6.

Cut the courgette, aubergine, peppers and onion into
1–2cm/½–1 inch chunks. Put in a large roasting tray
along with the tomatoes and garlic. Pour over the olive
oil, season with salt and pepper and toss together.

Roast for about 45 minutes, turning the vegetables a
couple of times throughout. Once they are all tender,
the cherry tomatoes have burst through their skins
and started to take on a golden edge, remove the tray
from the oven.

Squash the roasted garlic from its skin and gently stir
around the tray with the basil and balsamic vinegar.
Serve hot or cold.

Flexible

Chicken Ratatouille Traybake: *to make this into a main
course recipe, add 6–8 chicken thigh fillets to the tray and roast
for 15 minutes to get them started before adding the vegetables.
Continue to cook as above. You may need to split this between
2 trays if there isn't enough room for it all to sit in a single later.
Serve with pasta, cous cous, rice or Crunchy Smashed Potatoes
(see page 107).*

Pesto Cod Ratatouille Traybake: *once the ratatouille
has had 30 minutes cooking time, sit 4 chunky fillets of cod
(or other sustainable white fish fillet) on top. Spread each one
with 1 teaspoon pesto, scatter with grated Parmesan and return
the tray to the oven for 20 minutes until the fish and vegetables
are cooked through. Carefully lift the fish from the tray, stir
through the basil and balsamic vinegar.*

Cucumber, mango and peanut salad

Chunks of cucumber are a staple accompaniment on many children's plates at mealtime, as a nod to the fruit and veg quota for the day. However, it's pretty boring to have it on its own all the time. This salad may take a little longer to prepare than just cucumber, but it's far tastier, much more interesting, and even better for you than just cucumber on your plate.

---

1 cucumber
1 ripe mango
½ red onion, thinly sliced (optional)
1 tbsp rapeseed (canola) or olive oil
juice ½ lime
½ tsp caster (superfine) sugar
flaked sea salt
50g/1¾ oz roasted skinned peanuts

Time taken 15 minutes / **Serves** 4–6

Cut the cucumber in half lengthways and thinly slice each half on the diagonal into slim pieces. Put in a bowl.

Peel the mango and cut the flesh into thin slices a similar size to the cucumber. Add to the bowl.

Toss the onion, if using, into the cucumber and mango along with the oil, lime juice, sugar and a pinch of salt.

Roughly chop the peanuts and scatter over the top.

Flexible

Nut-free: *the peanuts can easily be taken out of the recipe altogether, or for those wanting them, simply scatter over individual portions when serving.*

Upgrade: *add some chopped red or green chilli, a small handful of chopped coriander (cilantro), mint or Thai basil and a splash of fish sauce for additional flavour and spice.*

Flexible tomato sauce

*A homemade tomato sauce is much
more nutritious than most bought
varieties. This recipe makes a pretty
decent-sized batch as it is best to make
plenty so you can store some in the
fridge to use during the week and keep
the rest in the freezer for later use.
Use for stirring into pasta, to top pizza
bases (see page 68), for pasta bakes/
lasagne or spooned over cooked fish,
meat or roasted veg. Or loosen it with
some vegetable stock to make a soup.*

---

4 tbsp olive oil
2 onions, finely chopped
2 sticks celery, finely chopped
2 carrots, finely chopped
2 courgettes (zucchini), finely chopped
4 cloves garlic, peeled and crushed
2 bay leaves
4 x 400g/14 oz tins of chopped tomatoes
2 tbsp tomato purée
large pinch of dried chilli flakes
  (optional)
1 tbsp balsamic vinegar
1 tbsp caster (superfine) sugar
handful basil leaves, chopped
flaked sea salt and freshly ground
  black pepper

Time taken 1 hour / **Serves** 12

Heat the oil in a large saucepan and gently sauté
the onion, celery and carrots for about 10 minutes
until softened. Add the courgettes, garlic and bay leaves.
Increase the heat and continue to sauté for 3–4 minutes.

Stir in the tinned tomatoes, tomato purée, chilli flakes,
if using, balsamic, sugar, basil and a good pinch of salt
and pepper. Bring to a simmer, cover loosely with a lid
and cook over a low heat for 30–40 minutes until the
sauce is rich and thick.

Use straightaway or store in the fridge for up to 1 week.
You can also divide the sauce into individual portions
and freeze for up to 3 months.

Flexible

Make it smooth: *blend to your preferred consistency with a
handheld blender, removing the bay leaves beforehand.*

Make it creamy: *blend silken tofu until smooth and stir
through the sauce for a protein-rich creaminess. Alternatively,
mascarpone, cream cheese or double cream can also be used.*

Puttanesca: *add 8 chopped anchovy fillets, 2 chopped red
chillies and 1 tablespoon dried oregano to the pan with the onion.
Stir in 2 large handfuls stoned and halved black olives and
5 tablespoons capers when you add the tomatoes.*

baking and desserts

Lemon and raspberry loaf

Think of this as a modern-day lemon drizzle cake. It's ideal for anyone who can't have dairy and is totally vegan friendly, you can even go gluten-free (see Flexible below). What I really want to make clear is that it tastes soooo good. The sponge is light, fluffy and exceptionally lemony, and the topping is wonderfully vibrant in colour. But it's the intense raspberry flavour that's the real showstopper. So, move over lemon drizzle, there's a new cake in town!

275g/9¾ oz self-raising (self-rising) flour

200g/7 oz caster (superfine) sugar

1 tsp baking powder

grated zest and juice of 2 large lemons

75ml/2½ fl oz/¹⁄₃ cup soya milk

100ml/3½ fl oz/scant ½ cup sunflower or rapeseed (canola) oil, plus extra for oiling

50g/1¾ oz fresh or frozen raspberries

100g/3½ oz icing (confectioners) sugar, sifted

1 tbsp freeze-dried raspberry pieces

Time taken 50 minutes / **Serves** 12

Preheat the oven to 200°C/180°C fan/400°F/gas 6. Brush a 450g/1 lb loaf tin with a little oil and line the base with baking parchment.

Mix together the flour, caster sugar, baking powder and lemon zest.

Put the lemon juice in a jug and top up with milk to 175ml/6 fl oz/¾ cup. Pour into the dry ingredients along with the oil. Mix to a smooth batter and pour into the prepared tin. Bake for 40 minutes, until the top is light golden, firm to touch and a skewer comes out clean when inserted in the middle.

Cool the cake for 10 minutes in the tin before removing and cooling completely on a wire rack.

To make the icing, blend the raspberries to a purée then sieve to remove the seeds. Pour the raspberry purée into the icing sugar in stages, mixing well after each addition until you reach a thick pouring consistency. Slowly spoon the icing on top of the cake, allowing it to drip down the sides, and scatter with freeze-dried raspberries to finish.

Flexible

Gluten-free: swap the flour to a gluten-free self-raising (self-rising) flour.

Flavour swap: use blackberries instead of raspberries for a lemon and blackberry loaf. Switch the lemon zest and juice for orange and make the icing using pomegranate juice and a splash of rosewater for an orange, pomegranate and rose loaf. Scatter with fresh pomegranate seeds to decorate.

Favourite chocolate brownies

I'm a huge fan of making brownies. You can be as flexible as you like with flavourings and treats added to the brownie mix, depending on what you've got in the cupboard or who you're making them for. Once you've made a batch you'll realise that this is a very flexible recipe that can be adapted for any occasion, from a bake sale, morning coffee, decadent dessert, a foodie gift, weekend baking with the kids or simply as a naughty-but-nice treat for the family.

200g/7 oz unsalted butter

200g/7 oz plain chocolate (about 70% cocoa solids), chopped

3 eggs

300g/10½ oz granulated sugar

2 tsp vanilla extract

125g/4½ oz plain (all-purpose) flour

pinch of flaked sea salt

Plus... additional flavours (optional)

1 tsp ground cinnamon or ginger

½ tsp chilli powder (believe me, it's delicious)

1 tbsp instant coffee dissolved in 1 tbsp hot water

grated zest of 1 orange

1 tbsp brandy, rum, coconut or orange liqueur

... and up to 250g/9 oz treat of choice (optional)

white, milk or dark chocolate chunks/chips/buttons

pecans, walnuts, toasted hazelnuts or macadamia nuts, roughly chopped

fudge or caramel chunks

dried fruit, such as cherries, raisins, cranberries

mini marshmallows (just a couple of handfuls)

fresh raspberries

chopped stem ginger or candied peel

Time taken 45 minutes / **Makes** 15 generous-sized brownies

Preheat the oven to 180°C/160°C fan/350°F/gas 4.

Line a 20 x 30cm/8 x 12 inch rectangular, 3–4cm/ 1¼–½ inch deep baking tin with baking parchment.

Place the butter and chocolate in a bowl over a pan of barely simmering water and leave to gently melt, stirring as little as possible. Alternatively, gently melt in the microwave in 10-second bursts.

In a separate bowl, whisk together the eggs, sugar and vanilla extract until they are lovely and thick and creamy, but you still feel the gritty granules of sugar. Pour in the melted chocolate and butter and mix in.

Sift in the flour and salt and add any optional flavourings or treats.

Pour into the baking tin and bake for 25 minutes until the top is cracking and the centre is just set. Leave to cool in the tin for about 30 minutes before cutting into squares.

Flexible

Gluten-free: *the recipe is just as perfect with a plain gluten-free flour.*

Dairy-free: *choose a suitable dairy-free chocolate and any treats. For a butter substitute you can use a dairy-free butter, coconut oil or even a light olive or sunflower oil. The results are a little softer and gooier but what's not to like about that!*

Creamy mango, passion fruit and lime pots

Serving up a dessert that's fresh, light, healthy and fruity is often tricky to find, unless of course it's a piece of fruit or flavoured yoghurt. This is where these come in. If you've not done it before, you'll be amazed at just how creamy cashew nuts become when they're blended with a little water. They make a brilliant dairy-free alternative to whipped cream. Because they're mild in flavour they make an ideal base to add fruit purées to, letting the fruit do all the talking.

125g/4½ oz cashew nuts
2 large ripe mangoes, peeled and stoned
grated zest and juice of 1 lime
2 ripe passion fruit
caster (superfine) sugar or agave syrup
    to taste, depending on the natural
    sweetness of the fruit (you may not
    need any at all)

Time taken 30 minutes + 2 hours soaking and 1 hour chilling /
Makes 4

Soak the cashew nuts in cold water for at least 2 hours, but overnight is fine.

Put the mango flesh in a blender or food processor along with the lime zest, juice and passion fruit pulp. If you prefer to remove the seeds, press the passion fruit pulp through a sieve first. Blitz to a purée. Have a taste and if the purée seems too sharp, then add a little sugar or agave to sweeten. It's likely you won't need any at all if the mangoes are naturally sweet enough. Remove half the fruit purée and keep to one side.

Drain the soaked cashew nuts and add to the fruit purée in the blender. Blitz really well, until you have a smooth thick creamy consistency. Continue to blitz if it still seems grainy.

Spoon the fruity cashew cream into glasses or dishes and spoon the remaining fruit purée on top, stirring gently to create a swirly, ripple effect. Put in the fridge to chill for at least an hour.

Serve the fruit pots with additional passion fruit pulp and grated lime zest on top.

Flexible

Nut-free: swap the cashew nuts for a thick coconut yoghurt (or Greek yoghurt if dairy is suitable). Stir through half the fruit purée rather than blending it, and spoon into glasses or dishes served with the remaining purée swirled on top.

Flavour swap: you can try all sorts of fruit combinations using soft fruits or fruit purées: 200g/7 oz raspberries; 1 banana and grated zest of 1 orange; 250g/9 oz cooked rhubarb purée and diced stem ginger; or 250g/9 oz blackberries and the grated zest of 1 lemon.

Cinnamon-sugared doughnut balls

OMG is the reaction my kids and friends gave when trying these for the first time. You really can't beat freshly made doughnuts, generously sprinkled with cinnamon sugar, eaten straightaway when they are still warm. I like to serve them with a dollop of raspberry jam (try Chia-Berry Jam, see page 28) to dip into. It's not essential but definitely adds to the heavenly experience.

300g/10½ oz plain (all-purpose) flour
125g/4½ oz caster (superfine) sugar
1 tbsp baking powder
pinch of flaked sea salt
2 eggs
225ml/8 fl oz/scant 1 cup milk
75g/ 2¾ oz butter, melted
1 tsp vanilla bean paste
sunflower oil, for deep frying
raspberry jam (optional)

For the cinnamon sugar
75g/2¾ oz caster (superfine) sugar
2 tsp ground cinnamon

Time taken 30 minutes + 30 minutes resting / **Makes** about 24 little balls

Make the cinnamon sugar by combining the sugar and cinnamon and set aside until needed.

Put the flour, sugar, baking powder and salt in a large bowl and mix together.

In a jug or separate bowl, mix the eggs, milk, melted butter and vanilla together and pour into the dry ingredients. Mix well to form a smooth batter and put in the fridge to rest for about 30 minutes.

If you have a deep-fat fryer, fill with oil and set to 180°C/350°F. Alternatively, pour a depth of 5cm/2 inches of oil into a large deep saucepan or a wok and heat to 180°C/350°F. If you don't have a thermometer to check the oil is hot, drop a cube of bread into the pan and it should be a deep, even golden within 40 seconds.

Working in batches, drop tablespoons of the batter into the hot oil. Use a small ice cream scoop if you have one to maintain equal-sized doughnut balls. Cook for about 4 minutes before carefully turning the doughnut ball over to cook evenly. It's well worth cooking one on its own first and cutting it in half when cooked to check the cooking time, as you want to make sure there isn't any raw dough in the centre.

Remove the doughnuts from the hot oil with a slotted spoon and drain on kitchen paper. Scatter generously with the cinnamon sugar while still hot. Continue until all the batter is used up. Serve the doughnut balls as they are or with raspberry jam for dipping.

Flexible

Gluten-free: you can swap the plain (all-purpose) flour for a gluten-free flour, but I suggest you mix it with 1 teaspoon xantham gum to give the doughnut balls a lighter consistency when cooked.

Dairy-free: swap the milk and butter for plant-based dairy-free alternatives.

Flavour swap: you don't have to stick with cinnamon sugar to sprinkle on the doughnut balls; how about making some lemon sugar? For every 200g / 7 oz sugar, blitz in the grated zest of 1 lemon in a food processor or spice grinder. It also works well with orange or lime zest.

Amazing chocolate chip cookies

We all need a simple go-to chocolate chip recipe that's crispy on the outside with chewy melty perfection on the inside… well, here you have it. I can't recommend these enough, they're easy to make, and you'd never know it but they are egg-, dairy- and nut-free, so suitable for various dietary requirements including being vegan.

300g/10½ oz plain (all-purpose) flour
1 tsp baking powder
1 tsp bicarbonate of (baking) soda
200g/7 oz milk or dark chocolate chips
  (dairy-free if required)
½ tsp sea salt
150ml/5 fl oz/⅔ cup olive oil
100g/3½ oz caster (superfine) sugar
75g/2¾ oz soft light brown sugar
1 tsp vanilla bean paste
60ml/4 tbsp cold water

Time taken 25 minutes / **Makes** 18

Heat the oven to 180°C/160°C fan/350°F/gas 4. Line a couple of baking trays with baking parchment.

Put the flour, baking powder, bicarbonate of soda, chocolate chips and salt in a large mixing bowl and stir to mix.

In a separate bowl, mix together the oil, sugars and vanilla with 4 tablespoons cold water until thoroughly combined. Pour this into the flour and stir until the dough just comes together without over-mixing.

Scoop 18 balls of the dough and place on the prepared baking trays, leaving some space between for spreading. Press each one down lightly to flatten a little. If you are not intending on baking them straightaway, put in the fridge or freeze and defrost before cooking.

Bake for 14–16 minutes until the tops are light golden and the edges crisping. The cookies will have risen but as they cool they start to flatten down, leaving a slightly soft centre when cool. Cool on the baking trays and enjoy warm or cold.

Flexible

Gluten-free: swap plain (all-purpose) flour for a gluten-free flour, and use gluten-free baking powder.

Fruit and nut cookies: add 100g / 3½ oz roasted hazelnuts, roughly chopped and 100g / 3½ oz milk or dark chocolate chips to the cookie dough.

Orange, cranberry and white chocolate cookies: add the grated zest of 1 orange and mix in 100g / 3½ oz dried cranberries (roughly chopped if large) and 100g / 3½ oz white chocolate chips to the cookie dough.

Double chocolate cookies: replace 40g / 1½ oz of the flour with 40g / 1½ oz sifted cocoa powder and mix 200g / 7 oz dark, milk or white chocolate chips into the cookie dough.

Get ahead: the cookie dough freezes well. Scoop or roll balls of dough and freeze in a single layer on a baking tray lined with baking parchment. Once solid, store all together in a freezer bag. Defrost and cook as needed.

Star biscuits

Time taken 25 minutes + 30 minutes resting / **Makes** about 20

These are called star biscuits for many reasons, firstly and obviously because of their shape, but they are also stars in the kitchen because of the way in which you can handle them. The biscuit dough is very robust as once made, you can't over-knead it. You can re-roll it as many times as required, which is particularly handy when kids are involved in helping! The dough can be stored in the fridge or freezer once made and then cooked on demand.

140g/5 oz ground almonds
125g/4½ oz granulated sugar
finely grated zest of ½ orange
1 tsp vanilla bean paste
25g/1 oz cocoa powder
25g/1 oz icing (confectioners) sugar
1 egg white

Put the almonds, sugar, orange zest and vanilla in a large bowl. Sift in the cocoa powder and icing sugar and mix together to combine.

Add the egg white and mix well until you have a smooth dough. Turn onto the worktop and knead lightly for a minute until smooth.

Shape into a disk, wrap in cling film and chill in the fridge to rest for about 30 minutes.

Preheat the oven to 180°C/160°C fan/350°F/gas 5 and line a baking tray with baking parchment.

Once rested, roll the dough between 2 pieces of baking parchment, to about 5mm/¼ inch thick. Use a 4–5cm/1½–2 inch star cookie cutter, or in fact any shape you fancy, to cut out the dough shapes. Bring together the trimmings, re-roll and continue until all of the dough is used.

Sit the cookies on the lined baking tray. They won't spread when cooking so you should get them all on the same tray. Bake for 12–14 minutes, until the bases are slightly crisp but the middles remain just a little soft. Remove from the oven and leave to cool. As they cool they will firm up even more. Store in an airtight container. They should stay crisp for up to 2 weeks.

Flexible

Vegan/egg-free: *swap the egg white for 1 tablespoon chia seeds mixed with 3 tablespoons cold water. Leave to thicken for 10 minutes before mixing into the dry ingredients. The biscuits will probably need a further 1–2 minutes of cooking time until they are firm on the base with the middle still a little soft. They will firm up more when cooling.*

Flavour swap: *add ½ teaspoon ground cinnamon, ½ teaspoon ground ginger and ¼ teaspoon ground cloves to the dry mixture, either with or without the orange zest.*

Get ahead: *once the dough has been made and wrapped up, it can sit in the fridge for up to 1 week (just check the use-by date on your eggs first). You can also freeze the dough once cut into shapes. If baking from frozen, add on a couple more minutes to the cooking time.*

Peach and raspberry 'panic' pudding

Rather than racing to the shops for a last-minute 'panic' pudding, take a look around your kitchen and you'll probably be able to whip up this tasty dessert with just a few basic baking ingredients and some long-life fruit. I use tinned peaches and frozen raspberries but you can play around with any fruit combinations.

This tastes great served warm, but is also good at room temperature. Serve with cream, ice cream, custard or yoghurt. Leftovers can keep for a couple of days in an airtight container.

250g/9 oz caster (superfine) sugar
200g/7 oz butter, at room temperature
3 eggs
125g/4½ oz plain (all-purpose) flour
125g/4½ oz ground almonds
1½ tsp baking powder
125g/4½ oz frozen raspberries
  (fresh can also be used)
240g/8½ oz tinned sliced peaches,
  drained

Time taken 1 hour 20 minutes / **Serves** 8–10

Preheat the oven to 180°C /160°C fan/350°F/gas 4.
Lightly oil or grease a 1.5 litre/2¾ pint ovenproof baking dish.

Beat the sugar and butter together until light and fluffy in consistency. Gradually beat in the eggs, until fully mixed in. The mixture may appear curdled but it will be fine.

Add the flour, almonds and baking powder and mix with a wooden spoon until you have a smooth batter.

Transfer to the baking dish and level off the surface with the back of your spoon.

Arrange or scatter the peaches and raspberries on top. They will start to sink into the batter, but don't worry they will rise again when cooking. Bake for 1 hour or until the top is golden and the centre of the cake is just firm.

Remove from the oven and serve hot or at room temperature.

Flexible

Nut-free: use desiccated coconut.

Gluten-free: use gluten-free plain (all-purpose) flour.

Dairy-free/vegan: use a dairy-free butter alternative that is suitable for baking.

Switch the fruits: try different fruit combinations with tinned and frozen fruits, such as blackberry and pear, pineapple and blueberry, or cherry (tinned or frozen) or even use some tinned fruit cocktail.

Switch the nuts: if you've not any ground almonds, you can use any nut and blitz them in a food processer until ground.

Chocolate meringue mousse cake

Five simple ingredients is all it takes to make this utterly gorgeous dessert. It's neither too sweet nor too rich, with a deeply chocolatey mousse-like centre, beneath a thin crackly layer of cocoa-dusted meringue. What's not to love?

I find this is a perfect do-ahead dessert as I can make it a few hours ahead or even the night before. It becomes more dense as time goes by, so any leftovers can still be enjoyed a couple of days later.

150g/5½ oz dark chocolate (about 70% cocoa solids), broken into pieces
150g/5½ butter
pinch of flaked sea salt
4 eggs, separated
150g/5½ oz caster (superfine) sugar
2 tsp vanilla bean paste

To serve
1 tbsp cocoa powder, to dust
fresh seasonal berries
crème fraîche or whipped cream

Time taken 1 hour / **Serves** 10–12

Preheat the oven to 160°C/140°C fan/325°F/gas 3. Grease and line a 20cm/8 inch springform or loose-bottom cake tin.

Melt the chocolate, butter and salt together in a bowl set over a pan of gently simmering water, or gently melt in the microwave in 10-second bursts. Set aside to cool slightly.

Whisk the egg yolks with two-thirds of the sugar and the vanilla paste until thick, pale and fluffy.

In a separate bowl, whisk the egg whites to stiff peaks, then add the remaining sugar a tablespoon at a time, whisking thoroughly between each addition, until you have a thick and glossy mixture that holds itself in stiff peaks.

Pour the chocolate and butter mixture into the whisked egg yolks and gently mix together with a spatula.

Gradually fold in the egg whites using a metal spoon, taking care not to knock out all of the air. Once all of the egg white has completely mixed in, spoon the mixture into your prepared cake tin.

Bake for 35 minutes until lightly crisp on top but slightly wobbly when you give the pan a little tap. Leave the cake to cool completely in the tin before carefully removing and transferring to a plate.

Dust with cocoa powder and serve cut into slices with fresh berries and some crème fraîche or whipped cream (that's been generously flavoured with orange liqueur is my personal favourite).

Flexible

Upgrade: *add 1 tablespoon brandy, rum, coconut or orange liqueur to the melted chocolate and butter.*

Flavour swap: *fold through 100g / 3½ oz finely chopped roasted hazelnuts before transferring to the tin.*

Sticky lemon and orange cake

This is a brilliant go-to cake when you have people of all ages to feed with varying types of dietary requirements. Whether its gluten-free, dairy-free or vegan, you can adapt the ingredients as and when you need to, and no matter what, the end result is always going to be sticky, citrusy and unbelievably moreish.

Slice up the cake and enjoy as a treat any time of the day, or serve as a dessert with fresh raspberries, a dollop of extra yoghurt and some pretty green pistachios scattered over the top.

175ml/6 fl oz/¾ cup olive or rapeseed (canola) oil

2 small lemons

2 small oranges

250g/9 oz caster (superfine) sugar

2 eggs

175g/6 oz Greek yoghurt

2 tsp baking powder

175g/6 oz plain (all-purpose) flour

Time taken 1¼ hours / **Serves** 8–10

Preheat the oven to 180°C/160°C fan/350°F/gas 4. Brush a 20cm/8 inch round cake tin with some of the oil and line the base with baking parchment.

Thinly slice one of the lemons and one orange into half moon shapes. Put into a small saucepan, removing any pips as you go.

Finely grate the zest and squeeze the juice of the remaining lemon and orange. Set aside the zest,and pour the juice into the saucepan. Add 100g/3½ oz of the sugar and 100ml/3½ fl oz/scant ½ cup water. Stir, bring to the boil and simmer for 5 minutes until the orange and lemon slices are tender. Remove the slices with a slotted spoon and boil the liquid until you have a loose syrup – about 6–7 tablespoons' worth. Remove from the heat and set aside.

Beat the oil, remaining sugar, eggs, yoghurt and reserved lemon and orange zest together, to give you a thin batter consistency. Mix the baking powder into the flour and then stir them into the batter. Pour into the prepared tin and level the surface with the back of your spoon.

Arrange the orange and lemon slices on top and bake for about 40–45 minutes until golden and a skewer comes out clean when inserted in the middle.

Slowly pour the syrup over the top of the cake, allowing it to soak in. Cool in the tin for 10 minutes before removing from the tin and cooling further. Serve warm or cool.

Flexible

Dairy-free: use a dairy-free yoghurt (coconut yoghurt is particularly delicious).

Vegan/egg-free: this works amazingly well, so please do give it a try. Substitute the eggs for 2 tablespoons chia seeds mixed with 6 tablespoons cold water. Let sit for 10 minutes until gelatinous before adding to the cake batter in the above recipe. Use a dairy-free yoghurt such as coconut yoghurt.

Gluten-free: use a gluten-free flour and baking powder.

Upgrade: add a stalk of rosemary to the pan when making the syrup, and arrange a few small leaves on top of the batter with the lemon slices.

Jamaican banana and caramel pudding

This indulgent and comforting pudding magically creates its own rich molten caramel and rum sauce when baking, sitting beneath a banana and coconut sponge. It's a real crowd pleaser, making it ideal to serve when entertaining, yet it is also quick enough to prepare that you can enjoy it as a mid-week treat.

Next time you have an overripe banana, don't throw it out, give this pudding a go. The riper it is the sweeter and more intense the flavour.

175g/6 oz self-raising (self-rising) flour

100g/3½ oz caster (superfine) sugar

1 tbsp baking powder

pinch of flaked sea salt

1 ripe banana, mashed

300ml/10 fl oz/1¼ cups fresh coconut milk

85g/3 oz butter, melted plus extra for greasing

1 egg

1 tsp vanilla bean paste

flaked sea salt

cream, ice cream or coconut yoghurt, to serve

For the caramel sauce

150g/5½ oz soft dark brown sugar

4 tbsp golden syrup

2 tbsp rum or coconut liqueur

250ml/9 fl oz/1 cup boiling water

Time taken 1 hour / **Serves** 6–8

Preheat the oven to 180°C/160°C fan/350°F/gas 4. Grease a 24cm/10 inch diameter, 8–10cm/3–4 inch deep baking dish.

Put the flour, sugar, baking powder and salt in a mixing bowl. In a separate bowl or jug, mash the banana until smooth. Add the coconut milk, butter, egg and vanilla. Beat until smooth, then pour into the dry ingredients and mix to create a thick batter. Pour into the greased dish and set aside.

To make the sauce, put the sugar, golden syrup, rum or coconut liqueur and boiling water in a small saucepan and gently bring to a simmer, stirring to dissolve the sugar. Remove from the heat and pour over the top of the pudding. It will immediately sink below the batter, which is fine.

Put the dish on a baking tray and bake in the oven for 40 minutes until you have a lightly risen golden sponge, which will be sitting on top of a delicious caramel sauce.

Spoon into bowls and serve with cream, ice cream or coconut yoghurt.

Flexible

Gluten-free: self-raising (self-rising) gluten-free flour can be used.

Dairy-free: use a dairy-free margarine / butter or coconut oil in place of the butter.

Vegan/egg-free: substitute the egg for 1 tablespoon chia seeds mixed with 3 tablespoons cold water. Leave to stand for 10 minutes before using.

Chocolate celebration cake

When it comes to a celebration, chocolate cake is always a popular choice to serve, but what happens when you have people with varying dietary requirements to think about? Do you create hard work for yourself and make them something different, give them something shop-bought or pretend you forgot altogether!? Well, let that be a thing of the past. This cake could be your saviour as it ticks all the dietary requirement boxes, but the most important thing is that it tastes AMAZING.

For the cake

500ml/17 fl oz/2 cups soya or almond milk

2 tsp cider vinegar

300g/10½ oz light muscovado sugar

150ml/5 fl oz/²⁄₃ cup sunflower oil or light olive oil

2 tsp vanilla bean paste

250g/9 oz self-raising (self-rising) flour

100g/3½ oz cocoa powder, sieved

½ tsp baking powder

½ tsp bicarbonate of (baking) soda

For the chocolate buttercream

200g/7 oz baking margarine, at room temperature

200g/7 oz icing (confectioners) sugar, sieved

200g/7 oz dark chocolate, melted (use dairy-free for a vegan cake)

To decorate

dark chocolate (use dairy-free for a vegan cake)

75g/2¾ oz dark chocolate, melted (use dairy-free for a vegan cake)

75g/2¾ oz white chocolate, melted (use dairy-free for a vegan cake)

Time taken 1 hour / **Serves** 10–12

Preheat the oven to 180°C/160°C fan/350°F/gas 4. Brush 2 deep 20cm/8 inch springform or loose-bottom cake tins with some of the measured oil and line the base with baking parchment.

To make the cake, mix the milk and vinegar together. Leave for about 5 minutes for the milk to curdle, then stir in the sugar, oil and vanilla.

Sift together the flour, cocoa, baking powder and bicarbonate of soda and mix briskly into the bowl of wet ingredients, to give a smooth, very loose batter. Divide the chocolatey cake batter between the prepared tins and bake for 30 minutes until the sponges are evenly risen, just firm to touch and a skewer comes out clean when inserted in the middle. Leave to cool in the tin before carefully turning out to cool completely.

To make the chocolate buttercream, beat the margarine and sugar together until really light and creamy. Mix in the melted chocolate until smooth and the buttercream becomes spreadable.

Spread a thick layer of buttercream on top of one of the cooled cakes, then sandwich the other sponge on top. Spread another thick layer of buttercream on top, then use the rest to cover the sides of the cake, smoothing with a palette knife and turning the cake as you spread for an even, smooth finish.

Use a vegetable peeler to shave the chocolate over the top of the cake. Fill a small piping bag with the melted chocolate and pipe drips around the rim of the cake allowing it to run down the sides. Use the remaining to pipe on the top surface of the cake. Serve once the chocolate sets and enjoy over the next few days.

Flexible

Gluten-free: use self-raising (self-rising) gluten-free flour and baking powder.

Celebration cupcakes: the cake batter can be poured into paper or silicone cupcake cases and baked for 15–20 minutes. You can also throw some dark, milk or white chocolate chips into the batter for an extra chocolatey sponge. Decorate with the buttercream and add coloured sprinkles for fun.

Salted caramel kisses

If you're in the mood for doing some baking then these melt-in-the-mouth vanilla and cinnamon biscuits, sandwiched together with a creamy salted caramel buttercream are a must. Using a piping bag with a star-shaped nozzle makes them look impressive, but it's not essential. You can always just scoop small balls of the biscuit dough onto a baking tray, and when they are cooked, spread on the buttercream with a knife. They won't look as fancy, but they'll still taste as just good.

For the biscuits

300g/10½ oz plain (all-purpose) flour
2 tsp vanilla bean paste
100g/3½ oz caster (superfine) sugar
100g/3½ oz butter
½ tsp ground cinnamon
2 eggs, beaten

For the buttercream

100g/3½ oz butter, at room temperature
100g/3½ oz icing (confectioners) sugar,
  sifted, plus extra for dusting
100g/3½ oz caramel sauce
½ tsp flaked sea salt

Time taken 30 minutes / **Makes** 18–20 biscuits

Preheat the oven to 180°C/160°C fan/350°F/gas 4. Line 1–2 baking trays with baking parchment

To make the biscuits, put all the ingredients in a food processor and pulse blitz until combined. This can also be done by hand if you've not got a food processor – it's not exactly difficult but a little messier and takes slightly longer.

Using a piping bag and large star-shaped nozzle, pipe 36–40 rosettes onto the prepared baking trays, leaving a gap between each biscuit to allow for spreading. Bake for about 15 minutes until lightly golden. Once cooked and cooled slightly, remove from the tray and cool completely on a wire rack.

To make the buttercream filling, beat the butter and sugar together until pale and creamy, then beat in the caramel sauce and salt until you have a smooth creamy buttercream. Transfer to a piping bag with a star-shaped nozzle and pipe a decent-sized blob of the buttercream onto the base of half the biscuits. Top with the remaining biscuits. Hide from wandering hands if you don't plan on them being eaten straightaway!

Flexible

Gluten-free: use a gluten-free plain (all-purpose) flour.

Upgrade: dissolve 1 tablespoon instant coffee in 1 tablespoon hot water, leave to cool and add to the biscuit mixture.

Flavour swap: replace 50g / 1¾ oz self-raising (self-rising) flour with 50g / 1¾ oz cocoa powder to make chocolate biscuits. For the buttercream, replace the caramel with 100g / 3½ oz chocolate and hazelnut spread. Dust with cocoa powder when assembled.

Flexible fruit crumble

This is a recipe that's flexible from the top to the bottom. The quantities I've given all serve six to eight people, though you can increase to serve more when required.

I don't usually bother measuring the fruit. I'll have a baking dish in mind that will be suitable for the number of people to feed, and add the fruit directly to the dish, filling it about three-quarters full. So, here are a few crumble topping suggestions, and a basic method to follow and adapt accordingly for a finished crumble.

Classic (nut-free)
350g/12 oz plain (all-purpose) flour
1 tsp baking powder
175g/6 oz butter, chilled and diced
100g/3½ oz caster (superfine), brown or demerara (raw) sugar

Rub the flour, baking powder and butter together until it resembles fine crumbs and stir through the sugar.

Oat and Nut
150g/5½ oz spelt or wholemeal flour
150g/5½ oz butter, chilled and diced
1 tsp ground cinnamon
75g/2¾ oz flaked almonds, crushed lightly in your hands
50g/1¾ oz rolled oats
100g/3½ oz soft brown sugar

Rub together the flour and butter until it resembles fine crumbs. Stir through the cinnamon, almonds, oats and sugar.

Coconut (vegan)
200g/7 oz plain (all-purpose) flour
50g/1¾ oz rolled oats
50g/1¾ oz desiccated coconut
150g/5½ oz coconut oil, chilled
100g/3½ oz coconut sugar or soft brown sugar

Swiftly rub together the flour, oats, coconut and coconut oil until it resembles fine crumbs and stir through the sugar.

Fruit Filling
675g–850g/1½–1 lb 14 oz prepared fruit, diced into bite-sized pieces, removing any stems, seeds or inedible parts where required
100–200g/3½–7 oz sugar (any is fine), depending on the sweetness of the fruit
juice of 1 lemon or orange (not all may be required)
1–3 tbsp cornflour, depending on the juiciness of the fruit
1 tsp ground spice, such as cinnamon, ginger or nutmeg

Time taken 1 hour / **Serves** 6–8

Preheat the oven to 180°C/160°C fan/350°F/gas 4. Grease a baking dish with butter or a dairy-free alternative.

Toss the prepared fruit with the sugar, lemon/orange juice, cornflour and any spices in a large bowl. Use more sugar and less juice when cooking with tart fruits, like rhubarb and blackberries, and less sugar but more juice for sweet fruits, such as peaches and plums. Use more cornflour with very juicy fruits like plums or frozen berries and less with firm fruits like apples.

Tip into the baking dish and scatter the crumble topping evenly over the top of the fruit. Bake for 25–40 minutes until the fruit juices are bubbling around the edges of the pan and the topping is golden.

Flexible

Fruity choices: you can go with whatever you like. Let the seasons or what you just happen to have in your fridge or freezer determine what you use, whether it's classic apple (using a combination of Bramley and eating apples, and a scattering of cinnamon), Summerberry (using fresh or frozen combinations and a little orange zest), plum or peach (great with a nutty crumble topping) or rhubarb (with some vanilla or orange zest).

Sweet coconut risotto

Oh hello... this is what I call comfort food. Eating a bowl of this is like getting a big hug from your loved ones. Rich, delicately coco-nutty and oh so creamy, you will not want this to end. Serve, as I have, with some sliced or diced mango and pineapple, lime zest, toasted coconut flakes and a spoon of coconut yoghurt for a tropical touch, or simply a big dollop of raspberry jam in the middle (try Chia-Berry Jam, see page 28) for a more classic rice pudding-style dessert.

650–750ml/24–26 fl oz/2¾–3 cups
  fresh coconut milk
20g/¾ oz coconut oil
150g/5½ oz risotto rice
3 tbsp caster (superfine) sugar

Time taken 25 minutes / **Serves** 4

Put the coconut milk in a saucepan. Gently heat until the milk almost boils. Remove from the heat.

Melt the coconut oil in a saucepan over a low-medium heat. Add the rice and stir around in the pan for a minute or so until the rice is starting to glisten.

Gradually add one ladle of the hot coconut milk at a time, stirring almost continuously and allowing the milk to be absorbed before the next ladle is added. It should take about 20 minutes or so for all the milk to be absorbed and the rice to be plump and tender, giving you a delicious thick and creamy risotto.

Remove the pan from the heat and stir in the sugar. Taste for sweetness, adding a little extra sugar if you prefer. Spoon into bowls and serve straightaway with your choice of toppings.

Flexible

Fruity: serve the risotto topped with mango, pineapple, summer berries, grilled plums, peaches or nectarines.

Chocolate: stir 50g / 1¾ oz dark chocolate, broken into small pieces, through at the end.

Sweet vanilla or lemon: you can swap the coconut milk for dairy milk and flavour the risotto with the zest of ½ lemon or 1–2 teaspoons vanilla bean paste.

Carrot cake traybake

with cream cheese frosting and pecans

Carrot cake is a well-loved classic. There are numerous failsafe recipes to turn to, but the basics are the same: grated carrots, oil, sugar, eggs, flour and spices. I've chosen to use a wholemeal flour for the nuttiness it provides and substituted some sugar with a mashed banana. The cream cheese frosting is a classic, but to make this cake a little bit different, I like to add some pecan brittle on top.

150ml/5 fl oz/²/₃ cup sunflower or
    rapeseed (canola) oil
1 ripe banana, peeled and mashed to
    a purée
125g/4½ oz soft brown sugar
2 eggs, lightly beaten
175g/6 oz self-raising (self-rising)
    wholemeal flour
2 tsp baking powder
1 tsp bicarbonate of (baking) soda
1 tsp ground cinnamon
¼ tsp ground allspice
½ tsp ground ginger
200g/7 oz finely grated carrots
75g/2¾ oz sultanas
25g/1 oz desiccated coconut

For the frosting
75g/5½ oz butter, at room temperature
1 tsp vanilla bean paste
125g/4½ oz cream cheese
225g/8 oz icing (confectioners) sugar

For the pecan brittle
100g/3½ oz caster (superfine) sugar
50g/1¾ oz pecan nuts, chopped
sunflower or rapeseed (canola) oil,
    for brushing

Time taken 1 hour / **Makes** 12–16 slices

Preheat the oven to 180°C/160°C fan/350°F/gas 4. Line a 20 x 30cm/8 x 12 inch rectangular, 3–4cm/1½–1¾ inch deep baking tin with baking parchment.

In a large bowl, mix the oil, mashed banana, sugar and eggs together until totally combined. Mix in all of the remaining cake ingredients and spoon into the prepared tin, levelling off the surface with the back of your spoon.

Bake for 20–25 minutes until the cake has risen, is firm but springy when lightly pressed and a skewer comes out clean when inserted in the centre. Leave the cake to completely cool in the tin.

To make the frosting, beat the butter and vanilla with an electric mixer until smooth. Add the cream cheese and beat for a minute or so before sifting in half the sugar. Mix at a low speed to start with so you don't end up with a cloud of icing taking over your kitchen, then increase the speed until it's mixed in. Repeat with the remaining sugar and beat until it is a light creamy texture. Keep in a cool place until needed.

To make the pecan brittle, line a baking tray with baking parchment and brush with a little oil. Place the sugar in a saucepan over a medium heat. Leave until the sugar is melted and turned deep golden, swirling the pan a couple of times, but do try and avoid stirring the sugar. Stir in the nuts and tip straight onto the prepared tray. Leave for a few minutes to set.

When the cake is cool, spread the frosting over the top and serve cut into pieces, decorated with shards of pecan brittle.

Flexible

Carrot cake conversions: *the cake mixture can be spooned into cupcake cases and baked for 15–20 minutes. Or if you want a classic round cake, then divide the mixture between two 18cm/7 inch round tins and bake for 20–25 minutes.*

Nut-free: *honeycomb is a fun alternative to pecan brittle. Line a 20cm/8 inch deep baking tin with baking parchment. Heat 200g/7 oz caster sugar and 5 tablespoons golden syrup in a pan over a low heat. Dissolve the sugar then increase the heat and simmer until you have an amber caramel. Stir in 2 teaspoons bicarbonate of soda then pour straight into the tin and leave until solid (about 1 hour). Break into chunks and decorate the traybake.*

Tropical ice pops

Time taken 15 minutes + 4–5 hours freezing / **Makes** 6–8

Celebrate the natural sweetness and all-round goodness of fresh fruit by blending it to a purée, adding a few extras and making your own personalised frozen ice pops. You can be super-flexible on what you choose and it's a great way of using up fruits before they deteriorate, extending their shelf life and reducing waste. If you're short of decent fresh fruits to use, make the most of already frozen ones or even tinned fruits in natural juice.

Once you've blended your fruit choices, always have a taste before pouring into ice-pop moulds to check the balance of flavour, adjusting when needed. You shouldn't require any added sweeteners, but if you do find something a little too sharp, add a little honey or agave.

Flexible

Adult upgrade: *why not experiment by adding a splash of your favourite tipple. Gin, vodka and rum all work very well with the tropical flavours. Do make sure you label the alcoholic ice pops in the freezer to avoid a mix-up.*

Fruity yoghurt pops: *fruit, natural, dairy or plant-based yoghurts can be mixed into blended fruits and frozen in the same way. As with the fruit ones, have a taste before freezing and adjust according to preference.*

Mango, passion and watermelon double decker

2 medium ripe mangoes, peeled, stone removed and roughly chopped
3 tbsp coconut water or fresh fruit juice
pulp of 2 passion fruit
250g/9 oz watermelon, roughly chopped and large pips removed
10–12 raspberries

Blend the mango and coconut water or fruit juice until smooth. Stir through passion fruit pulp and pour into 6–8 moulds, filling roughly halfway. Freeze for around 1 hour. Blend the watermelon and raspberries until smooth and strain through a sieve to remove any seeds if preferred. Pour on top of the mango passion layer and freeze for around 4 hours or until fully frozen.

Coconut, lime and pineapple

1 x 400ml/14 fl oz tin coconut milk
1 ripe banana, peeled and roughly chopped
150ml/ 5 fl oz/²/₃ cup fresh pineapple juice
grated zest of 1 lime

Blend everything together and pour into 6–8 moulds. Freeze for around 4 hours or until fully frozen.

Watermelon and kiwi

600g/1 lb 5 oz watermelon, roughly chopped and large pips removed
3 ripe kiwi, peeled and chopped
4 tbsp fresh apple or pineapple juice

Blend the watermelon until smooth and pour into 6–8 moulds, filling about ¾ full. Freeze for around 1 hour. Blend together the kiwi and apple or pineapple juice and pour on top of the watermelon. Return to the freezer and leave for around 4 hours or until fully frozen.

Raspberry and lychee

400g/14 oz tinned lychees
200g/7 oz fresh or frozen raspberries

Blend together the lychees with their juice, and raspberries until smooth. Strain through a sieve and pour into 6–8 moulds. Freeze for around 4 hours or until fully frozen.

dietary index

When recipe title is in italics, please refer to the Flexible section on that page.

VEGETARIAN

GLUTEN-FREE

DAIRY-FREE

NUT-FREE + SESAME-FREE

EGG-FREE

index

Thank yous

Huge thanks to the amazing team who have helped in getting this book from a mere idea to being up on the shelves and in people's kitchens. I've thoroughly enjoyed working with each and every one of you.

At Frances Lincoln Publishing, I am extremely grateful to my commissioning editors Jessica Axe, Cerys Hughs and Melissa Hookway, who collectively got the book moving forwards smoothly and enjoyably. Plus of course the brilliant team who make all of the editing, design, proofreading, indexing, production, marketing, sales and publicity happen so brilliantly. Thank you so much, all of you.

Shooting the book was, as always, one of my favourite parts in putting a book together. Malou Burger – you're an awesome photographer and kept us moving swiftly from shot to shot (to shot…!) – even when we ended up working by torchlight in our festive jumpers. Veronica Eijo, I can't thank you enough; you were on top form assisting me in getting the food prepared and shoot-worthy. Millie McLuskie, this was your first book shoot but I'm sure there will be many more to come. Jimi, your patience and attention to detail is second to none, and I still can't make tea as good as you do! Thank you also to Pip Spence for the props – they were spot on, and a big thanks to Enya Todd for the stunning illustration on the cover.

As ever, a massive thanks to my lovely agents Borra, Louise and Jan at DML.

Thank you to everyone who buys and cooks from this book. I hope you, your family and friends all enjoy the flexibility of the recipes.

Finally, a HUGE big thank you to my wonderful family. You are my harshest food critics and keep me on my toes but I love you all.

Happy Flexible Family Cooking!

Brimming with creative inspiration, how-to projects and useful information to enrich your everyday life, Quarto Knows is a favourite destination for those pursuing their interests and passions. Visit our site and dig deeper with our books into your area of interest: Quarto Creates, Quarto Cooks, Quarto Homes, Quarto Lives, Quarto Drives, Quarto Explores, Quarto Gifts, or Quarto Kids.

First published in 2020 by Frances Lincoln Publishing,

an imprint of The Quarto Group.
The Old Brewery, 6 Blundell Street
London, N7 9BH,
United Kingdom

T (0)20 7700 6700
www.QuartoKnows.com

A catalogue record for this book is available from the British Library.

ISBN 978 0 7112 5168 7
Ebook ISBN 978 0 7112 5169 4
10 9 8 7 6 5 4 3 2 1

Assistant food stylist	Veronica Eijo
Designer	Isabel Eeles
Photographer's assistant	James Matthew
Prop stylist	Pip Spence

Printed in China

MIX
Paper from
responsible sources
FSC® C008047

**The item should be returned or renewed
by the last date stamped below.**

Dylid dychwelyd neu adnewyddu'r eitem erbyn
y dyddiad olaf sydd wedi'i stampio isod.

To renew visit / Adnewyddwch ar
www.newport.gov.uk/libraries